W9-BCV-614

A PRACTICUM
Immanuel

Patricia A. Velotta

LIBERTYVILLE, ILLINOIS

Immanuel: A Practicum
Patricia A. Velotta

ISBN: 978-0-9834546-5-6
Library of Congress Control Number: 2011944363

Published by This Joy! Books—A Division of Three Cord Ministries, Inc.
1117 S. Milwaukee Ave., Suite A4, Libertyville, IL 60048
www.thisjoybooks.com

Editor: Ginny Emery
Designer: Mary Anne Pfitzinger
Photo Credits
  front cover photos:
    "Cute boy on swing" © Alptraum | Dreamstime.com
    "Fall Birch" © Mary Anne Pfitzinger. Used by permission.
  back cover photos:
    "Playground Swing" © Lane Erickson | Dreamstime.com
    Author's photo © Michael J. Velotta. Used by permission.
    "Fall Birch" © Mary Anne Pfitzinger. Used by permission.

Printed in the United States of America
First printing, 2011
20 19 18 17 16 15 14 13 12 11   1 2 3 4 5

To my husband, Michael J. Velotta,
for his unfailing love and heroic faithfulness to me.

Contents

Contents

The Joy of Receiving
Testimonies

I understand *Immanuel* primarily because I have received his healing for ten years through this approach. I continue to be committed to my healing work with *Immanuel* because I want to be free, I want all that Jesus has for me, and I want those closest to me to reap the rewards of my healing. I want to be able to coach others, and I want to love the Lord my God with everything I am. God has worked a great deal of humility, compassion, and wisdom into me as I've pursued the Truth. For the most part, I enjoy my inner life in peace and hope since Jesus became Immanuel to me. My church says, "You've really changed!" Is that as a compliment?

Pastor Patti Velotta

What an amazing privilege to have my eyes opened up to see the living Jesus through *Immanuel* prayer. He is alive and is always with me. To see his care and creativity for every detail in my life has been transforming. Seeing him as he really is has given me peace through troubling times and has helped me to not just cope with life, or to just get by, but to learn to live and feel and experience abundant life. I am learning his true character and because of that, I am learning my identity in him.

Bob W.

I have had years of prayer counseling and was not prepared for the depth and power of the healing touch of Jesus in *Immanuel*. When Pastor Patti prayed for me on two occasions, I experienced Jesus like I have never experienced him before. The fullness of who he is has left an indelible imprint on my spirit.

Mimi L.

For years I have been praying, "Father, I only want to do what you're doing and I only want to say what you're saying, and I know it's possible because Jesus did it and he is our model." Sounds good, doesn't it—only I didn't know how to bring it about. Praise God for *Immanuel*; this is the key to having that intimate life of sonship with the triune God. As I see Jesus, "Who was and is and is to come" (Revelation 1:4, 8; 4:8), I don't have to guess what Jesus would do; I see him and know. Guess what? He loves it! He so desires that we would come to him and sup (Revelation 3:20) with him and walk with him. I am not the person I was because I now see myself through the undefiled eyes of love; we are changed from glory to glory as we behold him (2 Corinthians 3:18). There are not words enough to describe the deep abiding healing and redemption that transforms me through this ministry.

Linda H.

After just a few sessions of *Immanuel* prayer, I started to see good fruit in my life. I had new depths of peace, strength, and trust. I found that my circumstances don't change but I am changed. I have started to look for and see Jesus in the day to day. He's really with me! I am learning how he sees me and feel more loved, secure, and accepted. I am finding how good he really is!

Julie W.

I have been receiving and giving *Immanuel* for ten years, and I find that I have more freedom, more self-confidence, and I'm happier. I have developed the faith and assurance that I can see Jesus, and these results are not just for me. As I am coaching others, it is such fun. It is such joy to watch as he changes lives and brings freedom and intimacy to everyone.

Suzi D.

I'd like to thank Pastor Patti for bringing *Immanuel* to our church. Perhaps because of my training as an architect, I am always dealing with solving problems and understanding how things work. So, I have to admit that my first reaction to the *Immanuel* teaching was: "What kind of hocus-pocus is this?"

Although I outwardly agreed to come to that first session, I was kicking and screaming on the inside all the way there. Following Pastor Patti's encouragement to meet weekly, over the last couple of months Jesus has continued to expose, give me insight into, and lighten the burden of various issues and situations in my life. I feel much freer and know a greater peace than ever before.

As encouraging as his healing revelations continue to be, the thing I'm really excited to tell you is that I now sense that Jesus is alive and wants to be an integral part of my life.

I have always been a loner, and I struggle with creating strong emotional ties. For years I have heard the teaching that Jesus is always with me. But until now, it has always just been words. I have never felt a personal connection with Jesus and probably believed that I never would. But, astonishingly, as each week passes he shows up!—demonstrating to "little (six foot five inches tall) insignificant me" that he is with me and will not leave.

Week after week, my apprehension that he won't show up has continually been proven wrong and has encouraged me to look forward to our next meeting. I feel his presence—he has become quite real to me—until I now want to be the individual he created me to be and to share in all that he has for me. Thank you, again.

Bruce K.

◈ Foreword

One of Pastor Patti's strongest qualifications for teaching and writing about the Immanuel Approach is that she faithfully applies these principles and tools in her own life. Another strong qualification is that emotional healing and increased intimacy with Jesus are consistently being released through her ministry. Pastor Patti is also a good teacher, and my observation is that she has a special anointing for teaching and ministering to people in certain streams of charismatic Christian culture.

Some have found Wilder and Coursey's *Share Immanuel* to be particularly understandable and usable, while others have found the way I present material regarding the Immanuel Approach to be especially easy to understand and apply. I anticipate that there will be still others who will find *Immanuel: A Practicum* to be the best fit for the way they think and work. I am expecting that this book will be used by the Lord to help many receive his rich blessings through the Immanuel Approach to emotional healing and to life.

Dr. Karl Lehman, M.D.
Author of *Outsmarting Yourself*

Preface

After ten years of practice in both receiving and coaching, I agree with Dr. Karl Lehman, the originator of the Immanuel Approach, that it is the safest, easiest, and most effective approach to inner healing. *But* it is so much more. Inspired by Jesus as an end-time gift to his bride, it develops intimacy between the immanent God and the object of his love, the church of Jesus Christ. The whole of Scripture and the Holy Spirit lead us into the amazing truth that Jesus has always been with us, will always be with us, and is with us—*and* that he is knowable through encounter.[1] That is, we can see him, hear him, feel him, taste him, and smell him in the Holy Spirit. Jesus can and does reveal himself to us. He is actually present with us in the here and now. We can learn to practice his actual presence with us, receiving him in our hearts and minds.

However, we are hindered by wounds, lies, and sin. One crippling set of lies is that Jesus cannot be found and does not want us to find him. *Immanuel,* one of God's names, means "God with us." It is a fitting name for an approach that removes the barriers to the knowledge of God in Jesus Christ. I find that continued encounters with the ever-present God line up with Scripture and bring an increase of peace and joy with every meeting. As believers in Jesus Christ and what he accomplished on the cross for us, we can all know him personally, intimately, and vitally.[2]

Immanuel: A Practicum is intended to help you know *how* to do Dr. Karl's Immanuel Approach.

Many of you have seen an *Immanuel* session or attended a seminar. You feel ready to do *Immanuel* (the Immanuel Approach) with those around you. Others of you may not have had that specific training, but one of the strengths of this approach is that Jesus does it, so you can jump in and have the thrill of watching the Master work. This handbook is a brief summary of practical tips and the general steps of an *Immanuel* session for those who are ready and willing to try it.

◈ Acknowledgments

It seems at first contradictory to have so many people to thank for such a small book, but in a way, this writing has been a group experience as it has the fingerprints of encouragers and triggers throughout my life.

First and foremost thanks go to my husband, Mike, and also Dr. Karl, both willingly and successfully used by God for my ongoing well-being. (Can I mention Pastor Charlotte Lehman here as a friend of mine, but mostly because of her wonderful support of Karl as his wife.)

Second, thanks go to my girls: Mary, Molly, and Emily for the joy and strength they bring us just by being who they are. To Evans and Kevin, husbands and dads extraordinaire, your maturity and many kindnesses have released Mike and me to do what we do without worry about Mary, Molly, and our six (darling) grandkids. Thank you. And while we're at it, thank you, Emily, for your valiant and persistent comittment to *Immanuel* intimacy and healing.

To Calvary Way International Fellowship, our church, thank you for all your support and letting go so that we can follow the Lord. To Suzi DeRose, who has faithfully done whatever needs to be done at church and at home for thirty-plus years and still is as beautiful as ever.

To my Joel's Well buddies, Dr. Paul and Donna Cox, and Larry and Jacqueline Pearson, who have believed in me, encouraged me, and welcomed me into their hearts.

To my many encouragers on this project: my confidant, Faye Verstraten; my promoter, Mimi Lowe; my prophetic encourager, Persis Tiner; my disciple and researcher, Julie Wieland; and my colleague Pastor Linda Hoyt.

For those who in the beginning made a place for me to share *Immanuel* with their groups: Dr. Paul and Donna Cox, Pastors Kevin and Molly Kiefer, Pastor Linda and Jim Hoyt, John and Ann Smith, Pastor Patricia Hughes, Jean Fulin, Pastors Paul and Jan Knight. There are others who have picked up *Immanuel* and run with it such as Bob Wieland, Pat Helder, Joan Sexton, the London gang, the New Jersey gang, the Collingwood gang and many others—all of you are a great encouragement to me.

I am very thankful for Ginny Emery who began This Joy! Books with vision and conviction. She edited the book with a great deal of expertise and wisdom while overcoming great personal circumstances. Here's to you, Ginny. To Mary Anne Pfitzinger, managing editor and creative consultant, who is as good as her title is long. Didn't she do a great job on the cover too? To the gifted Sheila Urban for your excellent job proof-reading, as usual. Thank you all.

As *Immanuel* spreads and grows throughout the body of Christ, may your rewards be many and may your contribution to the preparation of the Bride be remembered by grateful participants.

◈ Immanuel: A Practicum

If you've discovered that having access to Jesus in the Spirit (seeing, hearing, feeling, and so forth) has changed and enriched your life . . . [Having experience]

And you want to help everyone you know share in this Good News . . . [Having desire]

And you understand that the old wounds, lies, and sin that have formed barriers to knowing Jesus and have blocked intimacy with him can be discovered, forgiven, and healed . . . [Having understanding of the problem and solution]

And you are willing to give *Immanuel* to those you care about so that they can live in more righteousness, peace, and joy in the Holy Spirit . . . [Having willingness]

Immanuel is here, for you!

This book is primarily a training manual for coaches giving[3] the Immanuel Approach to others, based on their own understanding and their experiences receiving *Immanuel.*

1 Beginning Questions

Why the Immanuel Approach?

The Immanuel Approach (or *Immanuel*) to inner healing is unique in the way that it results in deep intimacy with God. It restores one's relationship with him by removing the barriers of wounds, lies, and sin that are consequences of unresolved trauma in one's past. I think that this approach is part of the times of refreshing that must be in place before Jesus is released to come for his bride.[1] Won't a bride "not having spot or wrinkle,"[2] love the Lord her God with all her heart, soul, strength, and mind (Luke 10:27)? As he removes the barriers, we are able to see[3] Immanuel for who he truly is and can respond to his love while being transformed into his image.[4]

Jesus is the healer and the prize. And because Jesus is the very present leader providing the direction and solution, virtually anyone can develop the faith to coach.[5] Dr. Karl Lehman who, with his wife Charlotte, has taught *Immanuel* to thousands, writes, "Charlotte and I have used a variety of emotional healing tools over the years, and in our experience, the Immanuel Approach (*Immanuel*) has been the easiest to use, the safest, and the most effective."[6]

Is Immanuel the Only Way to Go?

I personally have used and sought healing through a variety of healing approaches. I don't know exactly what they have done for me, but I know that every one has contributed to my well-being. For example, Dr. Paul Cox is a close associate of mine. I believe that I will always use his inspired generational deliverance prayers and see real fruit. So I am not saying *Immanuel* is the only way. Jesus can do *whatever* he wants, *whenever* he wants, and we don't even need to understand the whats, hows, and whys of his choice. When I was first saved, my husband, Mike, and I went to a church that sang highly theological hymns—all six verses. At the time I didn't understand, but nonetheless I wept from the beginning to the end of those dear old hymns, never suspecting that Jesus was healing me of something or other.

But nothing I have tried compares to *Immanuel* for removing the barriers to intimacy with him. And since I am slated to be part of the bride of Christ forever,[7] I think this revelatory approach to healing is end time appropriate for the intimacy it produces.

As a pastor, my concern and responsibility is the "chaste virgin" that Paul talks about.[8] I am part of the plan to present whole and healed people to Jesus. I find that restoring true intimacy with God accomplishes that task. Jesus does it all. I have many friends who are wonderful discerners, deliverers, prophesiers, healers, even life-skills coaches, but *Immanuel* brings something different, something necessary, something refreshing. If your goal as coach (C) is to facilitate inner healing, you are going to be sorely tempted to have Jesus work primarily through you and your gifts rather than through a direct connection with Jesus. Here is the new thing: let Jesus himself work directly with the receiver. Many Cs will be uncomfortable with letting go of the wheel, and it may not be pretty (at first),[9] but once the receiver (the person who comes for ministry, "R") is engaging with Jesus, C's attempts to lead will just get in the way. Once he is connected to Jesus, R will discover intimacy and healing in the direct encounter with Jesus, without additional intervention from C.

I often hear people say, "Oh, this is another tool in my tool belt, and I pull it out when and if I need it." When I hear that, I know they don' t really understand *Immanuel*. I've learned by example and by experience, *don't mix* the Immanuel Approach with other approaches in one sitting. Perhaps I can say it this way, if you start with *Immanuel* but don't end with *Immanuel*, you haven't done an *Immanuel*. Since Jesus is present, willing and vastly capable, why are you resorting to any tools in your belt? If R needs generational deliverance, provide another time to do it. That way you are not signaling to R that you think that Jesus can't or won't complete what he is doing in this prayer time. Your confidence in Jesus will communicate to R that, with the support of a C, Jesus will work directly with him. God designed us to be in community. We just work better that way.[10]

One question I'm frequently asked is, "Can't I do memory work with God alone at home?" While God can do that, he rarely does. The coach facilitates the process, while Jesus leads the direction and content of the session. When R works out loud with C, R is bringing things to the light and thereby into history.[11] Cs are essential for listening, attuning, evaluating, and reminding Rs to turn to Jesus. Like the chaperone on a date, C has an important function. It's just not at the wheel.

Are There Additional Resources Available?

Dr. Karl Lehman, who has taught me most of what I know about the Immanuel Approach, in addition to his book, *Outsmarting Yourself*, has a new website "to provide resources that will help the Immanuel Approach to spread and thrive in every possible way" (www.immanuelapproach.com). Dr. Lehman has spent over ten thousand hours writing a comprehensive collection of essays totaling over one thousand pages which he offers to the public for free on his home page. To view his complete collection of essays about how to effectively minister healing to the mind, brain, and spirit system, go to www.kclehman.com. You can order very helpful videos with examples of his *Immanuel* sessions at this site. Dr. Karl has a collegial relationship with Dr. Jim Wilder, one of the developers of the THRIVE Ministry. Working together, Dr. Jim and Dr. Karl have developed a variation of the Immanuel Approach that can be used in group settings, and Dr. Jim has found great success teaching this to the persecuted church around the world. Dr. Jim has also written a booklet, *Share Immanuel*, primarily for those who have been trained in the Immanuel Approach on the mission field. I am giving seminars on the Immanuel Approach, and others are beginning to do the same. It's like a good restaurant, worship CD, or book; you want to tell everyone who will listen. I hope reading this book will help you to try it out yourself.

2 Getting Started

How Do I Begin?

If you are willing to try when you don't know everything and you know you don't know everything, you are off to a good start. One of the wonderful things about the Immanuel Approach is that it's for anyone—lay people, professionals, and beginners—and everyone who is willing can do *Immanuel* with remarkable fruit. Remember, Jesus does all the hard work, and you get to watch his expertise. Whether you are receiving or coaching, watching the Master is fascinating and redemptive. Your strongest asset is being willing to let Jesus do all the hard work. "Do not fear, little flock, for it is your Father's good pleasure to give you the kingdom" (Luke 12:32).

Whom Do I Start With?

Start with a trusted friend, someone with whom you feel safe. Trade off coaching one week and receiving the next. Once you have received and coached, this book will begin making more and more sense to you. If it seems good to both of you and to the Holy Spirit, keep going and see where he takes you. Once you start, Jesus will bring others for you to coach informally. I encourage you to keep experiencing Jesus and his healing for yourself. In fact, I recommend that everyone who wants to help others to become more intimate with Jesus should have a commitment to receive *Immanuel* regularly. You will not only gain in the experiential knowledge of God and therefore freedom in yourself, but also you will earn authority to help others. I have received *Immanuel* from Dr. Lehman for over ten years and plan to continue on a weekly basis. I know Enoch finished,[1] but as long as I remain here, I know I haven't!

What Is the Setup?

Depending on your time constraints, allow one to two hours for each prayer time. I schedule hour and a half sessions because we can always stop early.

With that said, have tissues and a wastebasket handy. Almost everyone cries when they are deeply touched by Jesus. Some tears are relief, others are from various pains, still others are pure joy.

I don't insist on having an intercessor in the room, and most of the time I don't have one. However, I don't meet with R unless someone else is nearby, especially when I am coaching a man.

What happens in a session belongs to Jesus, R and C. At the start, I tell people three things up front:

1. Very occasionally, if I feel the need, I talk with my husband about a session—omitting unnecessary details.

2. I may talk with Dr. Karl Lehman as my advisor, mentor, and colleague about a session.

3. I ask permission to share some of the sweetest things Jesus says or does for illustrations and ministry.

This way, I make sure to provide a safe and caring place for Jesus to do his healing work. (*Jehovah Rapha* = I AM Healing.[2])

I *never* lead.[3] Well, I'd like to say that, but I keep trying not to take the wheel. After all, Jesus is really there and really wants to do something wonderful for both of you. When C commandeers the flow of the session, even by following what he thinks is Holy Spirit, look out! Jesus will let you take over, and in a short time you will be back to your old stand-by approaches, wondering where he went. Please let him do his job and be the Director, Discerner, and Deliverer. To put it bluntly, your job is to coach R to turn to Jesus for help and *not* to you.

What Does a Session Look Like?

These are the basic parts of any *Immanuel* session:

Greeting

Opening Prayer

Focusing on Jesus—Positive Memory, Appreciation, Locating Jesus in the Room

Memory Work

Healing

Closing Prayer

Conclusion

3   Greeting

Can C and R Talk?

I always take time to express that I am happy to see R. I like to talk a little before we work. This gives a friendly warmth to the time together and gets us settled. I also listen for clues about where Jesus might be taking R. Jesus might have given her a topic before the session, or she might be clueless. No problem— Jesus always has a plan, and we don't have to know about it until it unfolds in the ministry time. Be sure to let R know that you are tracking with her cognitively and emotionally. That's attunement. You are letting her know that you are with her.

What If R Is Really Upset?

When you're just getting started with *Immanuel* prayer, it's important to have all the safety nets in place. If a person comes in "on fire," with a painful or upsetting issue all stirred up, make sure to attune to them until they are able to calm enough to establish the positive connection with Jesus. With beginner coaches, this safety net needs to be in place in case R gets into something later in the session that you don't yet know how to handle. With this in place, if anything comes up that you don't yet understand or know what to do with, R can be led back to the positive connection with Jesus, and thereby end the session in a good place. Cs that are just starting out should not have Rs attempt to work with underlying traumas if they are not able to establish the initial positive connection.[1]

With more experienced coaches, when someone comes in "on fire," it is usually most efficient to proceed directly to the issue at hand. That is, you may need to skip the initial focusing on Jesus. So after the friendly greeting and opening prayer, ask her to go back to the painful picture and find Jesus. Coach R to allow Jesus to take her to the memory that is a root cause of her current distress, to find Jesus there, to access the facts and feelings of the memory, and to receive resolution and healing from him.

How Do I Prepare R for First Finding Jesus?

Before I read the opening prayer, I give R a heads up about what I'm going to ask for in the prayer. Something like this,

> "I'm going to be asking Holy Spirit to bring to mind a memory of when you and Jesus had a positive connection. When he brings a positive memory to mind, I'm going to ask you to describe the memory. Then based on that time of positive connection, I'm going to ask you to tell Jesus directly what you appreciate about him."

Then I say,

> "While I read this really long prayer, just catch the memory Holy Spirit is bringing forward."

4   Opening Prayer

Immanuel Opening Prayer and Parameters

Dr. Karl Lehman

Prayer for the Facilitator

"Lord, I humbly acknowledge that sin, wounds, and lies distort my understanding and hinder my ability to follow you. *(If, as coach, you are aware of being stirred up in any way at the beginning of the session, take a moment to silently acknowledge the specifics to the Lord.)* I ask for special grace during this time: please carry all my unresolved issues so that they do not get in the way."

Requests Pertaining to the Immanuel Approach

"Lord, remind [name of **R**] of times (he/she) has experienced your presence in special ways. Bring forward one of these memories of special connection, help (him/her) to reconnect with this experience of being with you, and stir up appreciation in (his/her) heart. Lord, we ask that you will also reestablish a living, interactive connection, right here and now, in the present, as the foundation for this _____ (session/ministry time/prayer time/time of emotional healing)."

Dealing with the Demonic

"Lord, as you and [name of R] are establishing an inter-active connection, I also ask that you appoint represen-tatives for all evil spiritual forces that are present.

"We command all evil spiritual forces to be bound to the representatives that the Lord Jesus has appointed. You will only manifest and communicate with each other as Jesus allows and requires, you may not assist each other in any way, and you must be cut off from all outside spiritual forces. You must now return to Jesus, and to [name of R], everything you have stolen from (him/her). You must be stripped away from, and release, every part of [name of R]'s mind. You must be stripped of all your schemes, plans, agendas, and orders, and lay these at the feet of the Lord Jesus now.

"Lord Jesus, we submit to you the issue of compli-ance. We ask that you would deal with all evil spiritual forces that fail to comply.

In the name of Jesus, we command all evil spiritual forces: at the moment you fail to comply, you will im-mediately go to the true Lord Jesus and deal with him directly.

General Introductory Prayer

"Lord Jesus, we stand together and affirm the truth in faith, that you are here with us and that you love us— that even as we speak, you are preparing the way in the spiritual realm for [name of R]'s forgiveness, deliverance, healing, and freedom. We thank you for, and release with our prayers, the victory you have already accomplished through your death and resurrection, and the healing you have already provided through your wounds.

"Lord, you know [name of R]. Call (his/her) whole mind and heart, call every part of (him/her) forward. Help every part of (him/her) to hear your voice and to know the truth about your heart and character—about your gentleness and your carefulness—so that (his/her) whole mind and heart can cooperate with your healing work. Guide every thought, image, memory, emotion, and physical sensation coming into [name of R]'s awareness, and I ask the same guidance for myself."

Do I Have to Pray This Whole Thing?

Yes, it's best to pray it all; it prepares both R and C, and it gives clear notice to any demonic spirit. This prayer is often revised as Dr. Karl receives new insights, so it is not set in stone, but it covers the necessary bases to clean out the room and puts the demonic hindrances out of the way. It also establishes some very important scriptural facts about healing.

What Is Special about This Prayer?

Prayer for the Facilitator

The airlines have it right. They tell you that when the oxygen masks drop down, put yours on before you try to help the dependent who is traveling with you. It's so refreshing to acknowledge your own weaknesses and give them to Jesus.[1] Being real brings trust, while calling on Jesus brings security.

Requests Pertaining to the Immanuel Approach

Using someone's name is music to their ears, and using someone's name is good practice; it will help your memory and remind you to use R's name during your time together.

Dealing with the Demonic

Standing and declaring is based on Jesus' authority.[2] Some have asked why I don't just bind and cast out every demon involved. Although I don't speak to the demons that may be present, they are able to give useful information (wrong impressions and lies).[3] That's why I ask Jesus to appoint a representative, then bind the others to his chosen representative, and disconnect them from any reinforcements outside. Finally, I always ask Jesus to back me up if they disobey. This stops any spirits that might interfere with the ministry.

Affirming Jesus' Victory

The prayer reminds R that Jesus has already done the work, and we are collecting on what is already finished.

Confirming Jesus' Guidance

Both the heart and the mind are engaged; the heart informs the mind of the truth. I am asking Jesus to guide every awareness and to assure R of Jesus' ways.

What If I Find Myself without the Written Prayer?

Pray a paraphrased version. I have done an impromptu *Immanuel* session wherever the Spirit has nudged me[4]—in airports, hotel lobbies, on the beach, in my car, and so forth. I don't always have the written version with me, but when I do have it, in the office or another scheduled place, I read this prayer every time. I find that it lets R know that I don't think more of myself than I ought to and that I need Jesus' help too.[5] It emphasizes several truths that I might need to remind R about during the session. If I need to stand in my authority in Christ, I can stand on the foundation already declared in the prayer.

5 Focusing on Jesus

Positive Connection Memory

Reading the prayer gives R time to let Holy Spirit bring up a memory. It's essential that R doesn't try to think up a great memory, but just simply receives the one the Spirit gives him. At the end of the opening prayer, I ask R to tell me about the memory Holy Spirit brought to mind. Usually R can receive the memory, but occasionally a memory of a special connection with Jesus is blocked. When this happens, I try to encourage R with reminders like:

"**It's not up to you,**"

"**Let Holy Spirit bring it forward,**" or

"**Your memory can be very natural and simple—just an impression or even an emotion when you felt connected with Jesus.**"

What Do I Do If There Is No Memory of Positive Connection?

In the rare instances when R can't seem to remember a time of positive connection to Jesus, I encourage asking Jesus for help. "**Jesus, I need help.**" If that doesn't work, I don't take over and think of another tool in my belt—since this is obviously not working. No, I always wait for Jesus and R to connect. Waiting is uncomfortable, but Jesus always does something unexpected. So if there's no memory after first asking, I can suggest R telling Jesus, "**I need more help.**" And if necessary after that, I suggest R ask, "**What's in the way?**" Be patient and expectant until R starts to receive. If R is stuck for a while and you remain calm and confident in Jesus' ability to do his healing work, he will come through. R (and you) will see him once again triumph where it appeared there was no hope. Every time he shows his good, kind, all-knowing, ever-present, brilliant, powerful, loving self, you and R will gain capacity in knowing the true Jesus. Some Rs get old memories, some get spectacular memories, and some get "I saw the rainbow and knew he was showing me his love" memories. It's all good. Take whatever a person gets, even if it makes little sense at the moment because whomever Jesus shows himself to be in the memory often relates to the work he has planned for that session. For instance, a man came in worried about so many loose ends in his job. He saw Jesus holding a tassel in his hand. Jesus took him back to a memory in which he felt exactly the same way—overwhelmed by uncontrollable circumstances. He received peace by focusing on Jesus, and then he remembered Jesus holding the tassel. A tassel is made up of loose ends, and Jesus was handling it and enjoying it. Before we asked, he had sent the answer.[1]

Appreciation

Encourage R to report *everything* R sees, hears, feels, tastes, and smells. After recounting their memory (remember, C only knows what R reports), encourage R to feel the feelings in the memory. Let R enjoy Jesus and the feelings of that memory. When the emotions of the memory are still fresh, it is time for R to tell Jesus what he appreciates about him based upon that positive connection. It helps to start with the phrase, "**I appreciate that you, Jesus, are** _____ " (loving, patient, kind, forgiving, tender, powerful, all-knowing, sensitive, and so forth). This transitions R from a self-centered place to a place of seeing Jesus. After R is finished, C can chime in on the appreciation too. There's enough wonder to go around. Now R is beginning to focus on Jesus. Complete connection with Jesus is our goal. Healing and perfect peace come when our mind is set on him.[2] It's at that point that Jesus overcomes the world.[3]

What's the Difference between Thanksgiving and Appreciation?

Thank-yous are essential, but unless they are directed to who Jesus is, they tend to be self-focused and event centered. So it is important for C to help R to recognize Jesus' character rather than simply thank him for what he has done for him. When we appreciate his character, the whole focus shifts away from ourselves onto Jesus. Expressing appreciation of his character based on what he has done, takes gratitude to a different level. So instead of saying, "Thank you for making the rainbow and letting me feel your love through that," I encourage words like,

Jesus, you are so precise that you planned the timing of that rainbow before I was born to demonstrate your love for me. I appreciate your kindness in knowing what would catch my attention and communicate love to me.

I find that it is more difficult and more intimate to appreciate character. Sometimes praise is compared to worship by defining praise as what he has done, and worship as about who he is.[4] Once you tune in to character appreciation, it's easy to appreciate the person of Jesus as well as be thankful for what he has done. And since Jesus remains the same when he is discovered in the memory work,[5] R is already prepared to trust this precise, kind, and loving person.

Why Is It So Important to Appreciate Jesus Out Loud?

I'm not a brain scientist, but Dr. Karl is. This is one good reason to get a copy of his book, *Outsmarting Yourself,* and learn about the physiology behind what I am sharing. When we appreciate someone out loud, we set our brains to receive from that person. For example: I'm going to a convention, and the main speaker is someone that I have gotten a lot from in the past. On the way I tell my friend in the car how much I appreciate this speaker and by the time we get to the convention, I'm wide open to receive from the speaker.

Appreciating others out loud sets our brains to receive from them. Insights like this, based upon brain science, are keys that have inspired Dr. Karl's work. They form the basis of the Immanuel Approach. In case someone might think that this is purely physiological or psychological, I want to say that the Immanuel Approach is 100 percent consistent with the Bible as well.

Locating Jesus in the Room

In the opening prayer, we asked Jesus to remind R of a positive connection with him as a way to reestablish a living interactive connection here in the present to serve as a foundation for this session. Remember that in both the Old and New Testaments God says, "I am with you always." "I will never leave you or forsake you." Remember Psalm 139! He is truly Immanuel,[6] God with us.

After speaking words of appreciation, R is prepared to perceive Jesus' presence. She has set her brain to receive from Jesus and is focused on him. **"Where is he?"** **"Jesus, please help me to perceive your presence with me."** *Everyone* I have worked with has been able to find Jesus or sense his presence in the room the first time they try.[7] Most people are afraid that they won't be able to. We are simply not taught that the eyes of our heart/understanding/imagination have been enlightened—as Paul prayed for every member of the Ephesian church (Ephesians 1:16–18). Hearing God and feeling God by the Spirit of Christ is commonly reported by Christians,[8] but why not seeing him?[9] The ability to see in the Spirit is given to every Christian at regeneration, when we're born of the Spirit.[10] We can activate in the spirit the same five senses (hearing, seeing, feeling, smelling, and tasting) that we know in the natural realm. Jesus told Nicodemus, "Unless one is born again, he cannot see the kingdom of God" (John 3:3b). Being born again gives you access to encountering, specifically seeing, the kingdom and the King.[11]

What's the Importance of Finding Jesus in the Room?

Being focused on Jesus here in the present stabilizes, affirms, grounds, orders, and connects R with his real Healer and Source[12] and puts C in the background. This vital connection with Jesus provides capacity—the ability to go with him wherever he might chose to take R—even into memories that hold wounds, lies, and sin in his past. Knowing where Jesus is in the room also gives a necessary safety net so that R can return to that positive connection if memory content separates him from Jesus, and it becomes too difficult to stay in the memory alone.

If R Doesn't Find Jesus Right Away, How Can I Help?

I have worked with Rs who do not have a scriptural understanding for Jesus' presence, but they still experience seeing him in the room. Some Rs feel his presence while others see him very clearly. If R has temporary difficulty seeing, encourage her to ask Jesus for help. **"Jesus, I need help."** If that does not seem to work, ask, **"Jesus, what is in the way?"** If R only senses Jesus in her heart or has a vague awareness of him generally in the room, I encourage R to ask to perceive him as a "person" as opposed to a "presence." Many people need permission and are able to focus on Jesus as a person once they get the OK to actually see him.[13] Suddenly they will report something like, "Oh, he's right next to me with his hand on my shoulder!"

If R Still Doesn't Find Jesus, How Can I Help?

Sometimes I ask, **"Where might he be?"** People respond with their impression—even a very vague one—and then I ask,

"**What is he wearing?**" To their surprise, they can describe his clothing, his stance, his mood, his beard and hair, what he is wearing on his feet, and so forth. Seeing in the Spirit is different than seeing in the physical world.[14] No, the revelation of Jesus usually isn't going to appear in the physical realm.[15] Just think how many of us know that we can perceive God speaking to us, but most of the time we won't describe it as an audible voice. Nonetheless, it's very real. In the same way, Jesus appears through our imaginations. Sanctified imagination[16] is the bridge to the supernatural. Revealing Jesus is a function of Holy Spirit[17]"—the spirit of wisdom and revelation[18] in the knowledge [experiential] of him [Jesus Christ]" (Ephesians 1:17). Jesus is really there!

Does Jesus Look the Same to Everyone?

Sometimes Jesus chooses to wear something other than his white robe. He can appear in anything from jeans and a blue shirt to a bathing suit. Some are often surprised when they see Jesus in something other than Sunday school garb; then again others express worry that he wears his white robe every time. I just remind R that Jesus can wear whatever he wants. Sometimes, Jesus may even appear in the form of an Aslan lion or a famous personality, like Fred Astaire![19] I pay close attention to how Jesus reveals himself because it often is a confirmation of the work that follows. After all, he knows the end from the beginning. "Declaring the end from the beginning, and from ancient times *things* that are not *yet* done, saying, 'My counsel shall stand, and I will do all My pleasure'"(Isaiah 46:10).

23

Can Every Christian Believer Get Better at Seeing in the Spirit?

If Rs don't understand the basics of spiritual growth, I explain that spiritual growth is a developmental process,[20] just like natural conception and growth. I try to remind them that babies cannot see clearly when they are first born. They practice seeing. I encourage Rs to practice because we actually get better and better at finding him. The idea that Rs *can see* in the Spirit, supported by the C's confident cheering that they *can see* in the Spirit, helps Rs to take courage and see.[21] This is big! It translates outside the room into practicing the presence of God in the car, at home, everywhere. The Rs and the Cs both grow in their realization that Jesus *is* always with us.

Is Jesus Just a Picture, or Is This a True Encounter?

Because this is a real-time encounter,[22] Jesus actually interacts with R. After R finds and describes Jesus in the room with her, I often encourage her to talk with Jesus. As an initial connection point, she might ask, "Jesus, what do you want me to know?" And Jesus actually answers! Most of us have been taught not to expect a clear answer to prayer right away. I find that every encounter with Jesus teaches us that Jesus is here, and he is quite willing to converse with us. In fact, he loves it! He died for it.[23]

Once a man about my age with a strong Bible background came to see me. I suspect that his visit was a brave and humbling thing to do. He focused on Jesus and described a positive memory connection; then he took time to appreciate Jesus, speaking out loud directly to him; next I encouraged him to look around the room for Jesus. While he searched, I reminded him of several Scriptures assuring him that Jesus is always with us. Finally, he looked up and burst into tears exclaiming, "I don't know why he is doing this." I asked, "What is he doing?" He told me that Jesus was standing right in front of him and smiling at him. I think that it might have been the last thing he expected, but Jesus often does things we don't expect. When I was a new Christian, a wise Bible teacher once taught me, "If the thought you're thinking is smarter than you, it's God." Jesus outsmarts us, delights us, and (understatement) is way ahead of us!

6   Memory Work

What Is the Importance of Memory Work?

If there is bad fruit there are bad roots. When we are not living the kingdom life of righteousness, peace, and joy in the Holy Spirit, wounds, lies, and sin are actively at work.[1] Memory work takes us back to the source and origin (roots) of our continuing distress (fruit).

For instance: your mom took you to the store (thirty-five years ago when you were four years old) and turned the corner of the aisle while you were fascinated with watching Barney and not your mom. You realized that your mom was nowhere to be found. Now, with your four-year-old insight, you decided that . . .

1) I am alone,

2) forever,

3) I am lost,

4) forever,

5) Mom is unreliable,

6) forever,

7) all adults are unreliable,

8) forever,

9) I am not precious,

10) I am a throwaway,

11) the world is a mean place,

12) I am not loved or loveable!

You felt abandoned, hopeless, sad, and confused. None of your feelings were based on truth. However, these wounding lies will live in you until the Truth comes to set you free.[2] They become the roots of misplaced painful emotions, which can cause over-reactions or wrong reactions to current situations. Now at thirty-nine years of age, you don't understand where these feelings come from, why you have them, or where they really belong. "Why do I feel so intensely lonely? I have a good husband and friends. I guess I will always feel this way." When Jesus appears as Immanuel, God with us, he takes you back to the grocery store and the memory from when you were four. You realize that he was with you even though Mom was not.[3] You were never alone. You finally see the lies and replace them with the truth. Jesus overcomes negative feelings with peace. He does not change what happened, but he overcomes your negative feelings with his presence.[4] To your surprise, you eventually stop feeling intensely lonely.

Most traumatic memories are from childhood, but some adults have horrific adult memories of war, abuse, betrayal, losing a child, and so forth. Jesus is able to heal the wounds from these overwhelming situations in the same way he heals childhood traumas. He is with the person, shows them the truth, and brings peace through his attunement.

After Focusing on Jesus in the Room, How Do Rs Get a Memory to Work On?

Jesus has a plan[5] for every *Immanuel* prayer time. R may be in the middle of something he wants to work on—like the anger, shame, and confusion he's feeling after the fight with his wife that morning. If so, start there. I encourage him to ask "**Jesus, take me to the source and origin of these feelings.**" If there is nothing stirring in R, we ask, "**Jesus, what do you want to do today?**" Often I verbalize the prayer, asking R to agree in his heart with it or to say the words out loud himself. As C, I constantly remind R that Jesus has the wheel of the session.

How Does R Enter the Memory?

When R first receives a memory, she may see or feel one detail or lots of details. I go with whatever R gets and *immediately* encourage her to find Jesus in the memory, reminding her that he is and always was with her. I ask questions like, "**Where is he? Is he standing or sitting? What is the look on his face? and Where is his attention?**" It is good coaching to focus R on Jesus *first* in every memory. When the presence of Jesus is established in two places—the room and the memory, again I encourage R to ask, "**Jesus, what do you want me to know?**"

It is Jesus, not R, who unfolds the pieces of the memory. *Trying* to recall an overwhelming memory from the past, one that we have buried, is impossible. It is Jesus who releases it to us—with our permission. He alone can let us know what really happened and reveal our true thoughts and feelings.

God designed a memory system with built-in protection. Dr. Karl explains it this way: God built our brains with a protection mechanism like the circuit breakers in our houses. When electrical wires get overwhelmed, the circuit breakers pop so that the house won't burn down. When we are overwhelmed by negative emotions, our emotional circuit breakers pop—that is, we forget, bury, or put away our traumatic material rather than going crazy. As little children, some situations overwhelmed us. We simply could not process them, but now, as adults with Jesus' help, we can. This is important because the feelings of a memory—the anger, sadness, disgust, or fear—remain long after the facts of a memory are no longer available to us. Jesus is there and is able to let us know the feelings and facts again. Sometimes Rs need to ask for each piece. I coach them to always keep looking at Jesus as best as they can.

What If R Is Afraid or Doesn't Want to Go?

Most memories that Jesus takes R into are not pleasant on some level; if they were they wouldn't need healing. At times R may be reluctant to explore a memory with Jesus. Good News! If R is unready or afraid, Jesus is never demanding.[6] There will be other days. Jesus seems to be fine about waiting until R is ready. He goes about building an ability and willingness to go with him. He does this in different ways. Sometimes Jesus will appear in a vision, and R will go with him somewhere safe, beautiful, even familiar. At other times, Jesus will answer the question, "**Jesus, what do you want me to know?**" with assuring words like, "I am always with you for good." Again he may take R's hand or put his hand on R's shoulder. I encourage R to take time to enjoy Jesus and let his love and compassion soak in. When Jesus does this, he is preparing R to go into a memory.

The ability to trust Jesus, by knowing him for who he really is, increases our emotional and spiritual *capacity*. The Christian life is all about building capacity. In this setting, increased capacity helps R choose to go into a dark place of memory with him. Jesus also builds capacity for intimacy with him. He loves to be with us. Another reason Jesus has for building capacity is to bring R into his good plans for his life.[7] "The people who know their God shall be strong, and carry out *great exploits*" (Daniel 11:32b).

What Is Capacity? Is It Grace?

The word grace has so much theological baggage and is so often misused that I use Dr. Karl's term *capacity*. Although capacity is something like enabling grace, it simply means *ability*. The greater the capacity, the greater the ability to accomplish something. When I was a little girl, our family vacationed with my great aunt who lived in southwest Michigan. The treat of the day was a root beer float (root beer with a scoop of ice cream mushed into it). The problem was that Auntie Alice kept her ice cream in the big freezer across the huge room downstairs in her big, dark, musty, really scary basement. To enjoy the treat of the day, somebody had to go down there, into the dark basement, and get the ice cream out of the freezer—which, as I remember, was just past the bald light bulb in the middle of the room, immediately above the string we had to pull sharply before we could see *anything*. I remember going down the long flight of stairs, hoping to find the string, the freezer, the ice cream, and to get out of there. Of course after getting the ice cream, I had to turn the light off and find the stairs in pitch-black darkness before scrambling up to the safety of the kitchen. It was all I could do. In other words, my capacity was pushed to the limit. In contrast, the situation felt totally different if my dad went with me. My capacity shot up tremendously when my dad would take my hand and walk me down those same terrifying stairs—with Dad there was "no problemo." It was his job to find the string and to wait for me to get the ice cream, in the light—with company. Then he turned off the light and helped me find the stairs—without incident.

Can R Grow in Capacity?

"I know whom I have believed" (2 Timothy 1:12b). Getting to know Jesus intimately builds R's capacity to face the most dif-ficult of hurts and wounds—*with him*. Knowing where he is in the present as well as in a memory will provide a safety net for the dark places that need healing.[8] If the memory gets too scary, R can lose Jesus in the memory. I bring R back to the present to get resettled with Jesus before returning to what-ever is happening in the memory and finding him there again. Building capacity is worth the time even if R doesn't imme-diately go to painful memories. In fact, some sessions may be completely given to capacity building through visions rather than memories. R will see him for who he really is and trust him more fully to heal and not hurt him in encounter after encounter. And as capacity grows, R will realize that Jesus does all things well (Mark 7:37). R can put his confidence in him. So when R senses inside that he is going to a scary place, R has a big, strong, all-knowing, gentle hand to hang on to.[9] It makes all the difference.

What Is Secure Attachment?

Secure attachment is a vital human need; it is designed to be met during early childhood by a loving parent or caregiver. This attachment is the ideal foundation for relationships. When parents fail to act positively, in ways that a child can count on, a child will feel insecure.[10] Secure attachment occurs if: 1) when I look for my parent, I can find him; 2) when I find him, he is always happy to see me; and 3) he is the solution to my problem.[11] In *Immanuel*, Jesus never fails to manifest himself, to show joy in being with R, and to provide the solution to R's dilemma. He is 100 percent consistent in both his character and his abilities. I have a secure attachment to Jesus when I know that: 1) when I look for him, I will find him;[12] 2) when I find him, he is always happy to see me;[13] and 3) he is the solution to my problem.[14] Most Rs experience wonder at his unflappability and his obvious joy at being with them. *Immanuel* encounters provide opportunities in the present as well as in the past for us to connect with the One who is always with us, is always happy to be with us and is always the solution to our problems. Establishing secure attachment with Jesus corrects the attachment wounds of our childhoods. It moves us from a fear-based life to a joy-based one. *Great fruit!*

What If No Memory Comes Forward?

If R reports that she is "stuck" and her mind is blank, I remind her that the human mind is never blank.[15] I encourage her to just report, without editing, whatever is on her mind—a hamburger, her mom, a lamp shade, feeling hot or sad or hearing an unidentifiable sound—if R has asked Jesus to bring a memory forward, then believe that he has and go for it. Sometimes, it's hard to recognize memories because they feel like they're from our own minds. When that happens, I remind R that we have just asked Holy Spirit to bring forward a memory. So, "Why not go with it as if God actually answers prayer?"[16] I encourage R, **"Try to say whatever words are in your heart—without editing."** I assure her that the answer to her prayer is right there. It's just that we don't recognize it. Again, once R begins to enter the memory, the first and most important thing is to find Jesus.

Why Is It Important for R to Keep in Touch with Jesus?

Keeping in contact with Jesus is vital to the healing process. By establishing his presence in the room before going to a memory, R sees that he can move back and forth between the room and his memory. Jesus is in both places. You've established a safety net for him. Now, when going into a memory with a scant amount of information (and possibly a negative feeling about the darkness in the basement), R has more capacity to stay with it. If the memory feels too difficult to continue, I encourage R to return to the present room and reestablish contact with Jesus. I might say, **"Is Jesus still in the chair or did he move?"** At some point I usually remind R that Jesus promised never to leave him or forsake him and that he is always with him. It seems that Jesus moves as close to R as R allows. He never transgresses R's will. Often, as the session proceeds and as R becomes more comfortable with his presence, Jesus comes closer to R. A session might start with the perceived presence of Jesus across the room and end with Jesus sitting right next to R.

Is There Any Difference between an Immanuel Encounter and Guided Imagery/Visualization?

I don't ask, "Is Jesus here?" or "Is he over there?" but "*Where* is he?"[17] I have the biblical evidence to know for certain that Jesus manifests personally to each one of us.[18] He says that he never leaves us. Therefore, I know he is here. Some might argue that he is here only "in my heart," but over and over again, Jesus has shown us exactly where he is, what he looks like in the Spirit— he even reveals his mood. This information, however, doesn't come through my suggestion. I don't ever lead an R by suggesting or by describing what Jesus looks like. I don't set a scene: "Jesus is on the beach with white sand and his hair is blowing in the wind and you are running toward him." That is guided imagery. Instead, I ask Rs to tell me what they are experiencing. I have no idea what Jesus will do, say, or look like. He surprises me. His appearance might be big or small; his beard might be full or he might be clean shaven. He may appear in a white robe or jeans and a sweatshirt. It is his choice and often is meaningful to Rs for their healing work. Once an R saw Jesus in tennis shoes. He had trouble accepting that Jesus would wear tennis shoes. I reminded him that Jesus picks his own wardrobe and that it probably was not a vain imagination, since it was such a surprise. At the end of the prayer time, Jesus invited this R on a run in a vision. It turned out that the R was a runner and running with Jesus produced peace and joy. Then we remembered that Jesus was wearing tennis shoes! What a confirmation that Jesus was truly in the room and that he knows the end from the beginning. Usually the encounter is fresh, surprising, and full of things unknown to either R or C.

What Are Cognitive and Emotional Circuits?

Emotional circuits carry the feelings of memories, while the cognitive circuits carry the factual content. If the memory is a normal memory, R will remember both cognitive and emotional data. However, it's been interesting to me to return to a memory that I remember and have Jesus reveal all kinds of details that I didn't understand or perceive at the time. The most important revelation is always his presence with me. I may remember being alone and helpless, but when Holy Spirit takes me back into the memory, I can easily find Jesus. In fact, it is usually easier for Rs to see Jesus in a memory than in the present.

Cognitive content is *knowing* the what, when, where, and why of the memory. It can be remembered or supplied by Jesus if your cognitive circuits are on. That is why R keeps asking **"What do you want me to know, Jesus?"** and **"Please help me turn on my cognitive circuits."** The picture comes into focus as Jesus brings the missing pieces.

Emotional content is *feeling* the emotions of the memory. When R is fully reliving a memory, she will feel happy, sad, frustrated, angry, scared, and so forth. If R knows she's angry in the memory, but does not feel the anger in the memory, then her emotional circuits are not all on. I encourage R to ask Jesus for help saying, **"Jesus, will you help me turn on all my emotional circuits?"**

How Do I Coach Someone
Who Is Afraid of Feeling the Emotions?

It is more common to have a cognitive memory without emotions than to have emotional memory without corresponding cognitive content. Often R will be able to report exactly what's happening, but feel nothing. As R asks Jesus to help, I encourage him to press in, knowing that the feelings will probably be uncomfortable. I might remind him, "**This may not be pleasant, but remember, it will only last for a moment.**" As I coach R to feel his feelings, I remind him that feeling his negative feelings is not the primary goal, but that feeling *all* his emotions also includes receiving the good feelings of Jesus' attunement.[19]

What Is the Importance of Inside and Outside?

R might not experience the emotional content of her memory because she is outside of herself in that memory. When R arrives in a memory, she can observe it from outside or can experience it from inside herself. If she is observing it from the outside, like a movie, she will be able to see what is happening to her, but she will not be able to reconnect with her feelings. If R reports that she doesn't feel anything, I ask if she is outside of herself. "**Do you see the memory like a movie, standing outside of the picture watching yourself in the scene?**" If so, I encourage R to make a heart decision to get inside of herself in the memory. Once inside, R will report a different perspective. Suddenly, R will probably feel her emotions as well as experience her senses. I've had Rs describe the actual feeling of wind blowing and vivid sensations of smells, textures and sounds. More importantly, R needs to feel the emotions of the memory.

What If R Still Can't Feel Anything?

First, I encourage R to ask Jesus for *more* help. "**Jesus, I need more help.**" This is not fancy, but it does the job. Sometimes when I'm R with Dr. Karl, I have to keep pursuing by asking this many times. The Bible says to keep on asking, seeking, and knocking, and it will be opened to you (Luke 11:9). Jesus said that if even an unrighteous judge ruled justly because a widow kept bothering him, surely God would answer his own who keep asking (Luke 18:2–8). Don't give up. The next thing R knows, he will start feeling the emotions of the memory *and* Jesus.

What Are Some Other Blocks to Healing?

Although the opening prayer scrubs out the demonic inter-ference in the room, very rarely a demon may fail to comply with Jesus' commands and try to disrupt R's concentration. It may cause a headache or make R sleepy. Holy Spirit will help you as coach to stand in your God-given authority and com-mand the disrupting demon to go directly to the feet of the true Lord Jesus. I have never experienced any resistance to this command. Banishing the demonic is easy because they have to obey you in Christ's authority.[20]

If resistance is coming from R, then telling her to quit resist-ing does no good. People do not have to obey you, and Jesus will not make anybody do anything they don't want to do in these sessions. Parts of R's mind may not want to relive a diffi-cult time. If this happens, the coach encourages R to ask, "**Jesus, what's in the way?**" And Jesus will answer. Suddenly, R will know what is in the way. She will report something like—she doesn't believe Jesus can or will do anything about the situation, or she thinks Jesus will be mad at her, or she's pretty sure Jesus won't show up. I always encourage R to talk with Jesus about her fears. Usually Jesus says something that increases R's capacity, and R immediately goes to her memory. But occasionally, R isn't ready, even after talking with Jesus. If this should happen, it's your job as C is to assure R that Jesus won't force her. C can remind R that since Jesus has proven himself trustworthy so far, it might be worth a try to go with him. Jesus will be his tender, kindhearted, gracious self to R. He knows what R has to overcome to go to the memory. Jesus will attune to her and use this opportunity to build capacity in R.

Here is an opportunity to bargain with Jesus. I know "them's fightin' words," but bargaining with Jesus opens the door for progress. Remember he invites us to reason with him, "Come now, and let us reason together" (Isaiah 1:18a). In one of my sessions, I had some inkling that the memory coming up wasn't going to be fun—at all. I didn't trust Jesus either. So Dr. Karl suggested that I make a deal with Jesus—only if he wanted to, of course. I said that I would be comfortable if Jesus would promise not to say anything if I allowed him to show up in the memory. He agreed! I felt safe—until I remembered that Jesus can communicate without words. So I asked if, when he came, he would also turn around so that I couldn't see his face. He agreed. Again I felt safe—but just for a minute. Then I thought I'd cement it by asking him if, while not talking and facing the other way, would he please be in another room? He agreed. Instantly, I was outside a garage door, but the door had a window.

Jesus was in another room, but I could still see him. He had his back to me, as promised, so that I couldn't see his face. I could see, however, that he was sitting at a workbench. He was leaning over and working on something. He didn't say anything, but as I watched, I realized that his shoulders were moving. Then somehow I knew. He was working on me at the workbench. And he was weeping over *me*. I melted at his attunement. The bargainer just can't outsmart him.

Can C Be a Block to Healing and Intimacy?

Yes, because it may be very hard for Cs at this point not to jump in with all the answers and try to add their own otherwise good ideas. We Cs can act as if Rs can't connect with Jesus and that we have to do it for them. I think of it this way: Jesus is on a date with someone (R), but he is spending more time and energy talking with the chaperone (C) than he is with his intended date (R). I don't know about you, but after a while, I'd want to leave the two of them alone with each other. If you are the coach/chaperone, be quiet. Don't interrupt the two of them.

Interrupting Jesus changes the ministry time from an Immanuel Approach to a coach-is-ministering method. Holy Spirit may give us ideas, but we need to submit them to Jesus instead of taking the wheel and getting off track. "The spirits of prophets are subject to the prophets" (1 Corinthians 14:32). Exercise spiritual discipline! *If* we stay out of his way, Jesus is quite able to bring everything to resolution on his own.[21]

Interruptions can take many forms. Once, for example, I was coaching with an intercessor who received a prophecy for R during the *Immanuel* session. The intercessor respectfully asked if he could deliver the prophecy. I reminded him that Jesus was already in the room and talking with R. I had to suggest that the intercessor wait until R and Jesus were done and then give the words to *confirm* the work Jesus did with R.

The desire to interrupt is natural to all of us because we want to help, but it may not be spiritual. Occasionally my role as pastor gets mixed up with my role as coach, and I am tempted to correct R's theology or behavior—as if Jesus doesn't notice or is being too slow. Don't do it! Become more and more aware of the spiritual duct tape—nudges by the Holy Spirit to keep quiet. Let Jesus go where he wants to go and do what he wants to do without your intervention or initiative.

We should be aware of the double-dare dilemma. Cs are often motivated by their desires to help and to serve God. Coupled with these godly motivations can be their familiarity and ease with developed, tried, and true ministry gifts and skills. Sometimes ministry may trigger a need in C to be important. All this makes it difficult for C not to take over. On the other hand, Rs may be passive. Why work when someone else will? Isn't this the ministry model[22] we are used to? So much of our ministry subtly teaches that Cs have the inside track to Jesus and are more spiritual than Rs. And in some cases, R may be operating from a three-year-old's perspective of responsibility. So Cs might find themselves fighting R's stuff as well as their own!

Here's a possible solution to the dilemma. Dr. Karl describes impressions that come to him while coaching a session by saying, **"The thought that's coming to me is . . ."** He simply tells what is happening to him instead of weighting his interpretation with divine authority by saying, "Holy Spirit is telling me," or "God says . . ." When, as C, you tell R what is happening to you, you can then submit your own impressions to Jesus by suggesting that R speak to Jesus about them. "**Jesus, what do you want to do about it?**" This way, Jesus remains behind the wheel, R is still in the front seat, and C stays in the back.

How Important Is Encouragement?

Dr. Karl always makes it a point to say somewhere in the session, "**It's good to be with you, Patti.**" I have learned from him how important it is for a C to double as a cheerleader by saying positives like, "**Strong work! You're doing a good job. Lord, give her grace and courage. This is good work, press in!**" Encouragement really helps Rs know that they are moving in the right direction.[23] Discouragement is not from Jesus. Occasionally, R will report something like, "Jesus says that if I would just read my Bible more, or work harder or be more loving, that everything would be OK." These words sound like the old tapes we play to ourselves, the "helpful adult." Jesus tells us to come to him, and he will give us rest,[24] not work. C can spot these easier than R, so when I hear these "helpful adult" suggestions, I encourage R to ask the true Lord Jesus, "**Jesus, is that you?**" Jesus will let R know.

What about Vows, Forgiveness Issues, Generational Curses, and So Forth?

If Jesus brings these up within the context of a memory, vision, or conversation, I encourage R to follow Jesus. So sometimes, R will realize that he wants to ask forgiveness for something he's seen in a new light. Occasionally however, after asking Jesus,

"**What do you want me to know?**" R will hear the words to a vow running through his head. Then as C, I follow Jesus and encourage R to take care of that with Jesus. If R is asking Jesus for forgiveness, make sure that he receives forgiveness directly from him and not through you. Remember, *Immanuel* is all about *their* relationship with each other. Occasionally, generational curses seem obvious. Then I often encourage R to do that work in another appointment especially designed for that purpose. Here again, Jesus can do anything he wants, whenever he wants, just keep in mind that the intimacy we are looking for is never between C and R. It is always between Jesus and R.

7   Healing

What Is Attunement?

> Attunement is an especially important form of interpersonal emotional connection. I am successfully *offering* attunement if I see you, hear you, correctly understand your internal experience, *join* you in the emotions you're experiencing, genuinely care about you, and am glad to be with you; and you have successfully *received* my attunement if you *feel* seen, heard, and understood, if you *feel* that I am *with* you in your experience, and if you *feel* that I care about you and that I am glad to be with you. (Karl Lehman, *Outsmarting Yourself,* p. 323, emphasis in the original)

I liken attunement to a tuning fork resonating at the same frequency as the instrument being tuned. When Jesus attunes to us in *Immanuel,* we know he is truly with us.

What Does Jesus' Attunement Feel Like?

Attunement feels like Jesus connects and understands. When R has her emotional circuits turned on and feels Jesus' attunement, R is aware that Jesus perfectly understands and perfectly cares. He *is* Immanuel—God *with* us! Suddenly, nothing else seems to matter.[1] Even the negative ramifications of a memory vanish when Jesus fills the screen. He has overcome the world in R by capturing R's full attention.[2] Even the wrongdoers in the memory who caused the initial pain receive forgiveness effortlessly as Jesus' compassion flows into R. Jesus becomes all important. Righteousness, peace, and joy in the Holy Spirit are restored.

Can Jesus Heal If the Circumstances Remain Negative?

A good example of Jesus healing in negative circumstances is Stephen's stoning in Acts 7. Stephen looks up and *sees* Jesus. He experiences Jesus' perfect attunement. He is not alone, *God-with-us* is there with him. He sees Jesus for who he is and becomes like him.[3] Stephen's response is the same as R's. He moves through forgiveness into compassion for those who are stoning him. "Lord, do not hold this sin against them" (Acts 7:60). When you consider all Stephen might have been thinking at that moment, even accusations against God, his response is amazingly Christlike, "Father, forgive them, for they do not know what they do" (Luke 23:34). But on receiving Jesus' attunement, the situation no longer matters. Jesus overcomes the world[4] (he fixes us, not the world), he defeats the works of the devil (wounds, lies, and sin),[5] and he brings us into wonderful intimacy with himself[6]—*despite the circumstances*. Again, the Truth sets us free.

What Does Healing Feel Like?

R experiences healing when she feels perfect peace within the memory and in the present.[7] R's face will usually reflect the amount of peace and joy she is experiencing. When a particular memory is healed, R will quit trying to fix the situation and rest in Jesus' attunement. Evidence that R has turned from herself and the world to Jesus will be increased righteousness, peace, and joy in R's life.[8] The original situation will not be changed, but R is. Jesus never changes history. What happened in the memory is true, but the interpretation is changed. The holes are filled. Wounds are healed. True selves are revealed.

If R feels better but not 100 percent peaceful, I encourage him to say something like, "**Thank you, Jesus, for what you've done, but I want more.**" Or, "**Jesus, what is in the way of the complete healing?**" When the healing is complete, R will always describe peace and feel finished. Lies will be silenced. The world will be "strangely dim" and R knows that Jesus was with him all the time. His total attention will be on Jesus. Once again Jesus will be the hero, the centerpiece, the amazing healer, the compassionate attuner. This place is territory fought for and gained. It belongs to R and Jesus. It is a real place that R can retrieve at any time, returning to that memory place and reliving the peace and victory with Jesus. Additionally, Jesus will have built into R more capacity for the next memory. He wants to heal!

How Do I Know Immanuel Produces Fruit?

The work of the Lord remains.

> Therefore, my beloved brethren, be steadfast, immovable, always abounding in the work of the Lord, knowing that your labor is not in vain in the Lord. (1 Corinthians 15:58)

As difficult as it is to believe, everyone I have coached through *Immanuel* reports a profound increase in their level of intimacy with Jesus. Many Rs had never encountered Jesus as he really is. Many Rs believed that intimacy was for a few super-spiritual ones—certainly not for them. Many believed that knowing Jesus was for heaven only.

Through the Immanuel Approach, unprecedented righteousness, peace, and joy become evident in most R's lives and relationships. Most Rs can understand the peace and joy of being with Jesus. They already know that "in Your presence *is* fullness of joy" (Psalm 16:11) and that "you will keep him in perfect peace whose mind *is* stayed *on You*" (Isaiah 26:3). But they might not fully expect his righteousness, which is being right with him and with others. Righteousness is also part of *Immanuel's* fruit. Although we are already justified by our belief[9] in his finished work on the cross,[10] he wants to restore all areas of fellowship in our lives.[11] When Jesus takes R back to memories, he wants to give "exceedingly abundantly above all that we ask or think" (Ephesians 3:20). He wants to restore all that has been stolen from us of his original intentions. He will shine his light on each situation and emotion.[12] We discover the real truth about him, ourselves, and the world.[13] Righteousness is recovered. Forgiveness, deliverance, healing, and freedom are lasting fruit. He fulfills his promise, "I will restore."[14]

Concrete proofs of Immanuel's love can be truly amazing. Physical healings are reported.[15] Addictions are broken;[16] phobias fixed;[17] personalities integrated;[18] financial blessings released;[19] abundant life made evident,[20] and birthrights are being fulfilled.[21] I know because I, and those I've worked with, are experiencing this fruit. Dr. Karl receives similar testimonies almost daily.

8 Closing Prayer

Immanuel Closing Prayer and Commands

Dr. Karl Lehman

Thank You

Start with whatever you want to pray at the beginning of the closing prayer. I always include a brief thank you to the Lord for his presence and protection during the session and for whatever progress and/or healing has come. We pray to the Lord. We do not pray to demonic spirits—we stand in the authority of Christ and tell demonic spirits what to do.

Closing Prayer

If unresolved issues remain, begin here:

> "Lord Jesus, we hold up to you these wounds (and/or issues) that have not yet been fully resolved. We ask that you would care for them, and that you would surround [name of R] with your loving presence. We ask that you would manage the level of connection and intensity, giving (him/her) the grace to remain aware of and connected to these wounds (and/or issues) at whatever level is best for your plans for healing.

Otherwise, begin here:

> "Lord Jesus, we claim this territory that [name of R] has brought under your authority and protection today, and

we ask you to please designate all demonic spirits that you want to remove at this time. In the name of the true Lord Jesus Christ, we command that all demonic spirits that the true Lord Jesus Christ has designated must now go immediately and directly to his feet. You will go bound. You will not touch or harm anyone or anything on the way. He will deal with you as he sees fit. You will never come back. You will never send anything in your place.

"We claim the truth in faith: Jesus Christ, on the cross, took on Himself every curse that could ever come against [name of R]. In the name of Jesus, we now command that every curse associated in any way with these issues that have just been resolved must now be broken, destroyed, and rendered powerless, null, and void.

"Lord Jesus, we ask you to cleanse with your light and your love every place that has been left empty by the enemy. We ask you now to fill these places with your Holy Spirit and with your living presence, so that [name of R] may experience your living presence abiding in (his/her) mind and heart, and walking beside (him/her) each day.

"We command all demonic spirits that have been allowed to linger for any reason—you must now be completely bound in and under the name and authority of the true Lord Jesus Christ. You will not touch or speak to [name of R] in any way except as the true Lord Jesus Christ specifically allows to provide information he wants us to have to facilitate his healing work.

"Lord Jesus, we ask you to send your angels to surround, protect, and encourage [name of R].

"We also ask that you come with any additional blessings you want to deliver—anything else you have prepared for [name of R] today. We gladly deliver, with our prayers, all of the blessings you have prepared for [name of R] today."

What Is Special about This Prayer?

Paragraph One

I thank Jesus specifically for what he just did with R. I mention how wonderful he is and how wonderfully he has done in the session. This helps remind R of what was just accomplished. Sometimes R doesn't realize how much healing was done, and it helps to underscore the significant parts of the victory.

Paragraph Two

When the issues of the session are not completely finished, I ask Jesus to take care of them and watch over R until they are finished. I point out this part of the prayer whenever Rs express disappointment or fear that they did not do well enough in the session. It's often a relief for worried Rs to know that provision for unfinished business has been anticipated and that enough other people don't finish every issue in one session to include this in the prayer.

Paragraph Three

Now that Jesus and R have defeated the enemy, taken territory, closed wounds, and brought truth to the darkness, there is no more legal place for the demonic to infest. This paragraph is giving them notice to leave.

Paragraph Four

R and C agree that Jesus has already taken every curse. Based on his work on the cross on R's behalf, we claim that territory as well.

Paragraph Five

In the place of demons and their curses, we invite Holy Spirit to settle in those emptied spots. We also pray that R will experience the light, love, and presence of Jesus.

Paragraph Six

Demons carry lies and speak them into our thoughts, infiltrating our thinking, and misguiding our minds. Demonic spirits may still be anchored to wounds, lies, bitterness, vows or other problems that have not yet been resolved. While we don't speak to the demons directly, we use information from demons that is linked with our memories. For example, demons of fear often accompany traumatic memories. Asking Jesus what we're afraid of often opens the door to truth. There's a story about a father teaching his son to hunt. When they see three vultures circling, the son asks if they should kill them. The father explains that if they kill the vultures, then they won't be able to find what is wounded or dead. In the same way, we use demons to find the lies and to identify the open wounds that need closing. When healing occurs, we simply remove them[1] because they have lost their legal right to be there.[2] For now, we ask Jesus to bind them for his purposes. That way, they cannot harm anyone but are useful to the process when commanded by Jesus.

Paragraph Seven

Here I usually pray for R and his personal concerns. Often I will mention his family, work, and his life direction.

9   Conclusion

How Do You End the Prayer Time?

If R has experienced a healing with Jesus, R may not want to chat with C but will want to spend more time with Jesus. I remind R that the wonderful feelings of his presence are accessible any time R wants to return to them. If R has not experienced a healing, I remind R that he has had an encounter with Jesus and additionally has gained capacity because he now knows Jesus better. I try to maintain contact at the end of the time together, at least eye contact, but if it's appropriate, a hug. I let R know that he has done well. This is a good time to agree on the next meeting together.

10 Epilogue: The Joy of Coaching

I love helping people. One thing I love about *Immanuel* is that people actually get better—there's tangible, measurable, remarkable fruit. So many mental health workers try to help but see little or no change over long periods of time. The Immanuel Approach very quickly moves the receiver from despair to hope, from lies to truth, from fear to joy.

Another aspect of *Immanuel* that I constantly take joy in is the conformity of this approach to Scripture. Time and time again, Holy Spirit whispers, "This is that." Jacob wrestling with Jesus, Hannah pouring out her soul to God, David realizing that his sin is against the Lord, and Jesus washing the feet of the disciples are a few examples of parts of *Immanuel*. Richard J. Foster in *The Renovare Spiritual Formation Bible* introduces the concept of the "with-God life" as a model for seeing the whole of Scripture as the unfolding story of God's plan to bring us into our loving relationship with our Creator.

As a coach, I get to see Jesus solve the receiver's distorted ideas of his past in ways that I could never rival. Every time I coach, I am amazed at his love for the receiver (and me). If the coach coaches in faith that Jesus can and will do his healing work, then he will see marvelous things. The little sermons, prophecies, discernment, and wisdom that I am always tempted to give pale in the glorious work Jesus puts into smoothing the wrinkles of his bride. Again, there is a time and place for what I do as a pastor (and I do all these things that pastors do), but here, in *Immanuel*, Jesus builds capacity by revealing who he really is and his desire to have an intimate relationship with the receiver.

Perhaps the best part of coaching *Immanuel* is getting to know Jesus and being part of his work. Every receiver shares him with me as part of the session, so I get to see him in action. I get to watch him demonstrate his creative, caring, fun, surprising, brilliant way of doing and being. I have fallen much more deeply in love with him and I have gotten to know him in so many life stories. WOW! What a privilege to watch him work, recreating his sons and daughters and bringing them into their birthrights. I wonder if it's anything like what Wisdom (Jesus) experienced when watching and working along side of Father God and Holy Spirit in Creation.

When He prepared the heavens, I *was* there,

When He drew a circle on the face of the deep,

When He established the clouds above,

When He strengthened the fountains of the deep,

When He assigned to the sea its limit,

So that the waters would not transgress His command,

When He marked out the foundations of the earth,

Then I was beside Him *as* a master craftsman;

And I was daily *His* delight,

Rejoicing always before Him,

Rejoicing in His inhabited world,

And my delight *was* with the sons of men.

    (Proverbs 8:27–31)

Appendices

Quick Directions for an Immanuel Session

Remember, you are always a coach, never the Savior.[1] You are a connector not The Connection. Once you start an *Immanuel* session, don't commandeer the session, but dial down and trust in the Lord. He never fails! Confidence in Jesus through real experience is your greatest asset! His goal with R is intimacy with himself, but inner healing is a necessary and wonderful by-product.

Greeting (C)

Opening Prayer (C)

Catch a positive memory from the Holy Spirit. (R)*

Describe the memory to the coach while you relive it. (R)

Appreciate Jesus' character aloud. (R)

Find him in the room. (R)

Ask Jesus, **"What do you want me to know?"** (R)

Listen for indications of wounds and lies (C)

Ask Jesus to take you back to their source and origin, their roots. (R)

Catch—without editing—whatever Jesus is showing you. (R)

Ask Jesus, **"What do you want me to know?"** (R)

Keep asking until the memory is fully formed. (R)

Check to see if R is inside of himself/herself or watching from outside like a movie. (C)

If R is outside, coach him/her to ask Jesus to help him/her enter the self seen in the memory. (C)

Check to see if both your cognitive and emotional circuits are on. (R)

Ask for help from Jesus if they are not. (R)

Continue to focus on Jesus for direction and answers until you experience perfect peace. (R)

Take time to enjoy the moment with Jesus. (R)

Closing Prayer (C)

Encouragement, Reschedule, Good-byes (C)

* Anything marked (R) can be encouraged by you, the coach.

Notes

Oft-Used Quotes for an Immanuel Session

Things the Coach Might Prompt the **Receiver** to Say

Jesus, please help me to perceive your presence.

Jesus, what do you want me to know?

Jesus, take me to the source and origin of these feelings.

Jesus, what's in the way?

Jesus, I need help. Jesus, I need more help.

Jesus, please help me turn on my cognitive and emotional circuits.

Jesus, is that really you?

Jesus, give me grace and courage.

Things the Coach Might Say

Good to see you, [name of **R**]

Just report what comes to you.

Try to get the words in your heart.

Strong work; good work; you're doing really well.

Does that sound true to you?

How do you feel? How does that make you feel?

The thought that's coming to me is . . .

Jesus will never make you do anything.

What do you want to do with Jesus' invitation?

Is it alright with you if I read the closing prayer now?

Notes

God with Us

Aside from being a name of God, Immanuel is his very nature. He is God with us. There's a wealth of information in Scripture indicating his caring involvement in our entire lives.

Read and Meditate on Psalm 139

For the Chief Musician. A Psalm of David.

O LORD, You have searched me and known me. You know my sitting down and my rising up; You understand my thought afar off. You comprehend my path and my lying down, and are acquainted with all my ways. For there is not a word on my tongue, but behold, O LORD, You know it altogether. You have hedged me behind and before, and laid Your hand upon me. Such knowledge is too wonderful for me; it is high, I cannot attain it.

Where can I go from Your Spirit? Or where can I flee from Your presence? If I ascend into heaven, You are there; if I make my bed in hell, behold, You are there. If I take the wings of the morning, and dwell in the uttermost parts of the sea, even there Your hand shall lead me, and Your right hand shall hold me. If I say, "Surely the darkness shall fall on me," even the night shall be light about me; indeed, the darkness shall not hide from You, but the night shines as the day; the darkness and the light are both alike to You.

For You formed my inward parts; You covered me in my mother's womb. I will praise You, for I am fearfully and wonderfully made; marvelous are Your works, and that my soul knows very well. My frame was not hidden from You, when I was made in secret, and skillfully wrought in the lowest parts of the earth. Your eyes saw my substance, being yet unformed. And in Your book they all were written, the days fashioned for me, when as yet there were none of them.

How precious also are Your thoughts to me, O God! How great is the sum of them! If I should count them, they would be more in number than the sand; when I awake, I am still with You.

Oh, that You would slay the wicked, O God! Depart from me, therefore, you bloodthirsty men. For they speak against You wickedly; Your enemies take Your name in vain. Do I not hate them, O LORD, who hate You? And do I not loathe those who rise up against You? I hate them with perfect hatred; I count them my enemies. Search me, O God, and know my heart; try me, and know my anxieties; and see if there is any wicked way in me, and lead me in the way everlasting.

Food for Thought

A. What does God alone know about you?

B. What do you know about God's thoughts toward you?

Compare Psalm 139 with Jeremiah 1:4–5

Then the word of the LORD came to me, saying: "Before I formed you in the womb I knew you; before you were born I sanctified you; I ordained you a prophet to the nations."

Food for Thought

A. What effect did these words have on Jeremiah?

B. Would you like God to speak to you of His plans for you?

Bible Word Studies Relating to Immanuel

Treat yourself to some wonderful Bible word studies. (See next section below.) Research some words like *abide, near, with you, dwell, tabernacle, presence, leave nor forsake.* Here are some of my favorites:

near

You are near, O LORD, and all Your commandments are truth. (Psalm 119:151)

But it is good for me to draw near to God; I have put my trust in the Lord GOD, that I may declare all Your works. (Psalm 73:28)

near *(continued)*

"Am I a God near at hand," says the LORD. (Jeremiah 23:23a)

Draw near to God and He will draw near to you. (James 4:8a)

Also see Psalm 69:18; Isaiah 55:6.

abide

And now, little children, abide in Him, that when He appears, we may have confidence and not be ashamed before Him at His coming. (1 John 2:28)

But He said, "Abide in Me, and I in you. As the branch cannot bear fruit of itself, unless it abides in the vine, neither can you, unless you abide in Me. I am the vine, you are the branches. He who abides in Me, and I in him, bears much fruit; for without Me you can do nothing. If anyone does not abide in Me, he is cast out as a branch and is withered; and they gather them and throw them into the fire, and they are burned." (John 15:4–6)

dwell

He who dwells in the secret place of the Most High shall abide under the shadow of the Almighty. I will say of the LORD, "He is my refuge and my fortress; my God, in Him I will trust." (Psalm 91:1–2)

tabernacle (Hebrew word for "dwell")

And I heard a loud voice from heaven saying, "Behold, the tabernacle of God is with men, and He will dwell with them, and they shall be His people. God Himself will be with them and be their God." (Revelation 21:3)

with you

And the LORD, He is the One who goes before you. He will be with you, He will not leave you nor forsake you; do not fear nor be dismayed. (Deuteronomy 31:8)

And lo, I am with you always, even to the end of the age. (Matthew 28:20)

He shall call upon Me, and I will answer him; I will be with him in trouble; I will deliver him and honor him. (Psalm 91:15)

Fear not, for I am with you; be not dismayed, for I am your God. I will strengthen you, yes, I will help you, I will uphold you with My righteous right hand. (Isaiah 41:10)

The Lord Jesus Christ be with your spirit. Grace be with you. (2 Timothy 4:22)

Also see: Isaiah 43:5; Jeremiah 1:8; 19; 15:20; 20:11; Matthew 18:20; Luke 1:28; 15:31.

presence

You shall hide them in the secret place of Your presence from the plots of man; You shall keep them secretly in a pavilion from the strife of tongues. (Psalm 31:20)

And he said, "My presence will go with you, and I will give you rest." (Exodus 33:14)

Seek the LORD and his strength, seek his presence continually! (1 Chronicles 16:11)

You will show me the path of life; in Your presence is fullness of joy; at Your right hand are pleasures forevermore. (Psalm 16:11)

Also see: Genesis 3:8; Psalm 105:4; Acts 2:28; Psalm 21:6; 140:13.

leave nor forsake

Be strong and of good courage, do not fear nor be afraid of them; for the LORD your God, He is the One who goes with you. He will not leave you nor forsake you. (Deuteronomy 31:6)

Let your conduct be without covetousness; be content with such things as you have. For He Himself has said, "I will never leave you nor forsake you." (Hebrews 13:5)

For Deeper Word Study . . .

A. Look up each of these words in an English dictionary. Then look them up in Greek or Hebrew concordance and other resources. (You can go online, too.)

B. Look up additional Bible references using these words. List them.

C. Consider: How are they used? What does this mean? Does their significance change for you?

Remind Yourself of His Presence

Continue to remember the reality of God's presence, think of him often, remind yourself that he is near during the day until you begin to become aware of him all the time.

APPENDIX 3: GOD WITH US

Notes

Notes

Experiencing God

Note: For additional information, see the teachings of Neville Johnson (www.lwf.org.au). He introduced me to the idea of a sanctified imagination, which became the jumping-off place for my own research and thinking.

We can know God intellectually, in our minds, and experientially, in our hearts and lives. Words used in the original languages of Scripture tell us this. In Old Testament Hebrew the word *yadah* denotes an encounter with the five senses. We can encounter God with our senses in both the physical and supernatural worlds. In New Testament Greek, *gnosis*, refers to intellectual knowledge, but *epignosis* refers to experiential knowledge gained through our senses. *Epignosis* makes a distinction between knowledge of the mind and what I call knowledge of the heart. Vine explains the difference this way:

> *epiginosko* [verb] signifies (a) to know thoroughly (*epi*, intensive, *ginosko*, to know); (b) to recognize a thing to be what it really is, to acknowledge . . . *epignosis* [noun] full and thorough knowledge, discernment, recognition. (Vine, *Expository Dictionary of New Testament Words*, 27)

> (a) to observe, fully perceive, notice attentively, discern, recognize (*epi*, upon, and *ginosko*); it suggests generally a directive, a more special, recognition of the object known than does *ginosko*; it also may suggest advanced knowledge or special appreciation . . . (b) to discover, ascertain,

determine . . . to take knowledge . . . *epignosis* is knowledge directed towards a particular object, perceiving, discerning, whereas *gnosis* is knowledge in the abstract. (Vine, *Expository Dictionary of New Testament Words*, 299)

Here are a few Scriptures with *epignosis*, "experiential knowledge."

As they did not like to retain God in their *knowledge*, God gave them over to a debased mind, to do those things which are not fitting. (Romans 1:28)

I pray that the God of our Lord Jesus Christ, the Father of glory, may give to you the spirit of wisdom and revelation in the *knowledge* of Him. (Ephesians 1:17)

Till we all come to the unity of the faith and of the *knowledge* of the Son of God, to a perfect man, to the measure of the stature of the fullness of Christ. (Ephesians 4:13)

I pray that your love may abound still more and more in *knowledge* and all discernment. (Philippians 1:9)

We do not cease to pray for you, and to ask that you may be filled with the *knowledge* of His will in all wisdom and spiritual understanding; that you may walk worthy of the Lord, fully pleasing Him, being fruitful in every good work and increasing in the *knowledge* of God. (Colossians 1:9–10)

That their hearts may be encouraged, being knit together in love, and attaining to all riches of the full assurance of understanding, to the *knowledge* of the mystery of God, both of the Father and of Christ. (Colossians 2:2)

And have put on the new man who is renewed in *knowledge* according to the image of Him who created him. (Colossians 3:10)

Always learning and never able to come to the *knowledge* of the truth. (2 Timothy 3:7)

For if we sin willfully after we have received the *knowledge* of the truth, there no longer remains a sacrifice for sins. (Hebrews 10:26)

Grace and peace be multiplied to you in the knowledge of God and of Jesus our Lord, as His divine power has given to us all things that pertain to life and godliness, through the *knowledge* of Him who called us by glory and virtue. (2 Peter 1:2–3)

For if these things are yours and abound, you will be neither barren nor unfruitful in the *knowledge* of our Lord Jesus Christ. (2 Peter 1:8)

For *epignosis* I like to substitute the word *encounter* because it suggests knowing through the senses, experiential knowledge. In an encounter, I experience by seeing, hearing, touching, smelling, and tasting. Try reading these passages with *encounter* for a better understanding of what the authors were trying to say. Let's take Paul's prayer for every believer in Ephesus:

> I do not cease to give thanks for you, making mention of you in my prayers: that the God of our Lord Jesus Christ, the Father of glory, may give to you the spirit of wisdom and revelation in the *encounter (knowledge)* of Him, the eyes of your understanding being enlightened; that you may know. (Ephesians 1:16–18)

Here are other translations and paraphrases of *epignosis* in this passage.

Fuller knowledge—*The Twentieth Century New Testament*

Intimate knowledge—*The Centenary Translation: The New Testament in Modern English*

To know more of Him—*The New Testament in Modern English* (J. B. Phillips)

A growing knowledge—*The New Testament: A Translation in the Language of the People* (C. B. Williams)

In knowing him personally—*The Message*

In the recognition of him—*1898 Young's Literal Translation*

Paul is asking the Father of the Lord Jesus to give us the Holy Spirit for an encounter with Jesus. He links the Spirit of wisdom who shows the heart with the Spirit of revelation or understanding who tells the mind. (See endnote to appendix 4.)

The Greek word Paul uses for understanding is *dianoia* meaning "imagination, mind, and understanding."

> *Dainoia* denotes the faculty of thinking; then of knowing; hence, the understanding, and in general, the mind, and so moral reflection; it is rendered "imagination" in Luke 1:51 *(negative)* "the imagination of their heart" signifying their thoughts and ideas. (Vine, *Expository Dictionary of New Testament Words*, 248)

Because imagination can be negative, often denoting fabrication and fantasy, I refer to the positive and godly use of *dianoia* as "sanctified imagination."

Through the Spirit, the eyes of our imagination connect with the spiritual realm. Paul's use of *dianoia*, translated as *imagination*, in Ephesians 1:16–18, suggests that dianoia/imagination, is the word used in Scripture for that part of us that receives revelation; perhaps it is even the bridge between soul and spirit.

Imagination can be used for good or evil. *Dianoia* appears in thirteen passages: Matthew 22:37; Mark 12:30; Luke 1:51; 10:27; Ephesians 1:18; 2:3; 4:18; Colossians 1:21; Hebrews 8:10; 10:16; 1 Peter 1:13; 2 Peter 3:1; 1 John 5:20. In nine of these passages, including Ephesians 1:16–18, it is positive. The other four have negative connotations.

One positive use is Jesus' command to love God:

> So he answered and said, "'You shall love the LORD your God with all your heart, with all your soul, with all your strength, and **with all your mind** *(dianoia)*,' and 'your neighbor as yourself.'" (Luke 10:27) See also Matthew 22:37; Mark 12:30.

Jesus' wording seems redundant if soul is defined as intellect, will, and emotions. Yet it isn't redundant if the meaning of *mind* or *dianoia* is "imagination." If it is "imagination," it makes complete sense to love the Lord with everything you are: heart/spirit; soul or intellect, will, and emotions; mind/understanding/imagination; and strength/body.

Vain, empty, evil imaginations out of an evil heart block the knowledge of God.

> He has shown strength with His arm; He has scattered *the* proud in the imagination *(dianoia)* of their hearts. (Luke 1:51)

> [They] became **vain in their imaginations** *(dialogismos)* and their foolish heart was darkened. (Romans 1:21b, KJV)

> Because, although they knew God, they did not glorify *Him* as God, nor were thankful, but became futile in their thoughts, and their foolish hearts were darkened. (Romans 1:21)

We are to reject these vain imaginations.

> Casting down **vain imaginations** *(logismos)* and every high thing that exalts itself against the knowledge of God, bringing every thought into captivity to the obedience of Christ. (2 Corinthians 10:5, KJV)

> Casting down arguments and every high thing that exalts itself against the knowledge *(gnosis)* of God, bringing every thought into captivity to the obedience of Christ. (2 Corinthians 10:5)

A good, positive, sanctified imagination out of a pure heart has inspired thoughts. If imagination actually may be the bridge we use to receive revelation, when a sanctified imagination pictures God, it may be seeing God by the Spirit of revelation. "Blessed are the pure in heart, for they shall see God" (Matthew 5:8).

Paul prays that our spiritual eyes or imagination be "enlightened." Our word for photograph comes from this Greek word, *photizo*. "*Photizo* from *phos*, light . . . (b) used transitively, to enlighten, illumine" (Vine, *Expository Dictionary*, 31). Seeing with spiritual eyes may include seeing a picture by means of imagination. Jesus says that we must be born again (born of the Spirit) to see the kingdom of God.

> Jesus answered and said to him, "Most assuredly, I say to you, unless one is born again, he cannot see the kingdom of God." (John 3:3)

The Old Testament Hebrew word for mind in Isaiah 26:3 is *yetser* which means "form, frame, purpose or imagination." "You will keep him in perfect peace, whose mind is stayed on You, because he trusts in You. Trust in the LORD forever, for in YAH, the LORD, is everlasting strength" (Isaiah 26:3).

Yetser comes from the root *yatsar. Yatsar* means to "fashion, form, frame or make."

> *Yetser* "a form; (figurative) conception (i.e. purpose): frame, thing framed, imagination, mind, work. . . . This word also carries the connotation of something thought of in the mind, such as wickedness in people's hearts

(Genesis 6:5); or something treasured or stored in the heart" (1 Chronicles 29:18). (*Hebrew and Greek Key Word Study Bible NASB*, 1983)

God wants us to see into the supernatural with our spiritual eyes, that is, our sanctified imaginations, so that we might intimately know, experience, and encounter Him in our hearts and not just have head knowledge. God wants us to walk in the light, in the whole truth of who He is.

O house of Jacob, come and let us walk in the light of the LORD. (Isaiah 2:5)

Then Jesus spoke to them again, saying, "I am the light of the world. He who follows Me shall not walk in darkness, but have the light of life." (John 8:12)

We Are to See the Father

For he [Moses] endured as seeing Him who is invisible. (Hebrews 11:27)

For David says concerning Him: "I foresaw the LORD always before my face, For He is at my right hand, that I may not be shaken. . . . You have made known to me the ways of life; You will make me full of joy in Your presence. (Acts 2:25, 28)

He who has seen Me has seen the Father; so how can you say, "Show us the Father"? (John 14:9)

We Are to See the Son

Looking to Jesus, the author and finisher of our faith. (Hebrews 12:2)

A little longer and the world will see Me no more, but you will see Me. Because I live, you will live also. (John 14:19)

We Are to See the Spirit

The Father . . . will give you another helper . . . the Spirit of truth whom the world cannot receive, because it neither sees Him nor knows Him; but you know Him, for He dwells with you and will be in you. (John 14:16–17)

Our birthright is to be like Jesus. To be like him, we must know him for who he is.

For whom He foreknew, He also predestined *to be* conformed to the image of His Son, that He might be the firstborn among many brethren. (Romans 8:29)

Beloved, now we are children of God; and it has not yet been revealed what we shall be, but we know that when He is revealed, we shall be like Him, for we shall see Him as He is. (1 John 3:2)

Therefore, we are to grow and to be fruitful in the experiential knowledge of God.

Grace and peace be multiplied to you in the knowledge of God and of Jesus our Lord, as His divine power has given to us all things that *pertain* to life and godliness, through the knowledge of Him who called us by glory and virtue. . . . For if these things are yours and abound, *you* will be neither barren nor unfruitful in the knowledge of our Lord Jesus Christ. (2 Peter 1:2–3, 8)

Seeing God is normative Christianity. Paul prays for the whole congregation in Colossae as well as in Ephesus:

That you may walk worthy of the Lord, fully pleasing Him, being fruitful in every good work and increasing in the *knowledge of God*. (Colossians 1:10)

As followers of Jesus Christ, He is our model for living in the Spirit. He lived by imitating his Father who is in heaven.

Then Jesus answered and said to them, "Most assuredly, I say to you, the Son can do nothing of Himself, but what *He sees* the Father do; for whatever He does, the Son also does in like manner. For the Father loves the Son, and *shows Him* all things that He Himself does; and He will *show Him* greater works than these, that you may marvel. (John 5:19–20)

Jesus lived by the same Spirit that lives in us. While on earth he put down his transcendent God abilities of omnipresence, omniscience, and omnipotence and lived in the Spirit as a human being. We are to live in the Spirit also:

Let this mind be in you which was also in Christ Jesus, who, being in the form of God, did not consider it robbery to be equal with God, but made Himself of no reputation, taking the form of a bondservant, *and* coming in the likeness of men. (Philippians 2:5–7)

But if the Spirit of Him who raised Jesus from the dead dwells in you, He who raised Christ from the dead will also give life to your mortal bodies through His Spirit who dwells in you. (Romans 8:11)

If you think seeing, hearing, feeling, tasting, and smelling in the Spirit are only for superstars, the Bible tells us that we are all alike.

Elijah was a man with a nature like ours, and he prayed earnestly that it would not rain; and it did not rain on the land for three years and six months. (James 5:17)

Then Peter opened *his* mouth and said: "In truth I perceive that God shows no partiality." (Acts 10:34)

God gives various gifts, talents and callings, but he wants all of us to know, experience, and encounter him.

We Can Hear His Voice

The LORD thundered from heaven, and the Most High uttered His voice, hailstones and coals of fire. (Psalm 18:13)

To Him who rides on the heaven of heavens, *which were* of old! Indeed, He sends out His voice, a mighty voice. (Psalm 68:33)

To him the doorkeeper opens, and the sheep hear *his voice*; and he calls his own sheep by name and leads them out. (John 10:3)

Therefore, as the Holy Spirit says: "Today, if you will hear His voice, do not harden your hearts." (Hebrews 3:7–8)

We Experience Him through the Sense of Touch

And suddenly there came a sound from heaven, as of a rushing mighty wind, and it filled the whole house where they were sitting. Then there appeared to them divided tongues, as of fire, and *one* sat upon each of them. And they were all filled with the Holy Spirit and began to speak with other tongues, as the Spirit gave them utterance. . . . "For these are not drunk, as you suppose, since it is *only* the third hour of the day. But this is what was spoken by the prophet Joel: 'And it shall come to pass in the last days, says God, that I will pour out of My Spirit on all flesh; Your sons and your daughters shall prophesy, Your young men shall see visions, Your old men shall dream dreams.'" (Acts 2:2–4, 15–17)

Many in the Old Testament were touched by God.

Now when He saw that He did not prevail against him, He touched the socket of his hip; and the socket of Jacob's hip was out of joint as He wrestled with him. (Genesis 32:25)

And he touched my mouth *with it*, and said: "Behold, this has touched your lips; Your iniquity is taken away, and your sin purged." (Isaiah 6:7)

Then the LORD put forth His hand and touched my mouth, and the LORD said to me: "Behold, I have put My words in your mouth." (Jeremiah 1:9)

Many in the New Testament experienced Jesus' touch and were healed.

Then Jesus put out *His* hand and *touched* him, saying, "I am willing; be cleansed." Immediately his leprosy was cleansed. (Matthew 8:3)

Also see: Matthew 8:15; 9:20–22, 29–30; 14:36; 17:18; 20:34; Mark 1:41–42; 5:27–34; 6:56; 7:33–35; Luke 5:13; 7:14–15; 8:43–47; 22:51.

We Can Know Him through the Sense of Smell

Now thanks *be* to God who always leads us in triumph in Christ, and through us diffuses the fragrance of His knowledge in every place. For *we are* to God the fragrance of Christ among those who are being saved and among those who are perishing. To the one we are the aroma of death *leading* to death, and to the other the aroma of life *leading* to life. And who *is* sufficient for these things? For we are not, as so many, peddling the word of God; but as of sincerity, but as from God, we speak in the sight of God in Christ. (2 Corinthians 2:14–17)

And What about Taste?

> How sweet are Your words to my taste, sweeter than honey to my mouth! (Psalm 119:103)

> Your lips, O my spouse, drip as the honeycomb; honey and milk are under your tongue; and the fragrance of your garments is like the fragrance of Lebanon. (Song of Songs 4:11)

(Note: Many Bible scholars recognize the man in Song of Songs as Jesus and the woman as his bride, the church, or part of the church, depending on your theology.)

> Oh, taste and see that the LORD is good; blessed is the man who trusts in Him! (Psalm 34:8)

We can experience, with all our spiritual senses, deep, daily fellowship with God when we open to him.

> I have set the LORD always before me; because He is at my right hand I shall not be moved. (Psalm 16:8)

> Behold, I stand at the door and knock. If anyone hears My voice and opens the door, I will come in to him and dine with him, and he with Me. (Revelation 3:20)

†Endnote: The seven spirits of God, the Holy Spirit, are mentioned several places in Scripture. See also Revelation 3:1; 4:5; 5:6.

The Spirit of the LORD shall rest upon Him, the Spirit of wisdom and understanding, the Spirit of counsel and might, the Spirit of knowledge and of the fear of the LORD. (Isaiah 11:2)

God the Father sends the Spirit (in cooperation with Jesus and the Spirit).

But the Helper, the Holy Spirit, whom the Father will send in My name, He will teach you all things, and bring to your remembrance all things that I said to you. (John 14:26)

It's the Holy Spirit who reveals Jesus (in cooperation with Jesus and the Father).

Can you search out the deep things of God? Can you find out the limits of the Almighty? (Job 11:7)

He [the Spirit] uncovers deep things out of darkness, and brings the shadow of death to light. (Job 12:22)

But God has revealed them to us through His Spirit. For the Spirit searches all things, yes, the deep things of God. For what man knows the things of a man except the spirit of the man which is in him? Even so no one knows the things of God except the Spirit of God. (1 Corinthians 2:10–11)

Therefore, we cannot find out who God is without God's gracious revealing of himself through his Spirit.

Jesus answered and said to him, "Blessed are you, Simon Bar-Jonah, for flesh and blood has not revealed this to you, but My Father who is in heaven." (Matthew 16:17)

The specific work of the Spirit in Paul's prayer for the Ephesians is to enlighten our spiritual eyes so that we can see/know Jesus.

And He who loves Me will be loved by my Father, and I will love him and manifest Myself to him. (John 14:21b)

That I may know Him and the power of His resurrection, and the fellowship of His sufferings, being conformed to His death. . . . I press on that I may lay hold of that for which Christ Jesus has also laid hold of me. I press toward the goal for the prize of the upward call of God in Christ Jesus. (Philippians 3:10, 14)

Notes

People in Scripture Who Saw God

I've had so much fun looking up the people who saw God in the Bible. Maybe you can think of some I missed.

People in the Old Testament Who Saw God

1. Adam and Eve

And the LORD God caused a deep sleep to fall on Adam, and he slept; and He took one of his ribs, and closed up the flesh in its place. Then the rib which the LORD God had taken from man He made into a woman, and He brought her to the man. (Genesis 2:21–22)

2. Cain and Abel

And in the process of time it came to pass that Cain brought an offering of the fruit of the ground to the LORD. Abel also brought of the firstborn of his flock and of their fat. And the LORD respected Abel and his offering. (Genesis 4:3–4)

3. Enoch

After he begot Methuselah, Enoch walked with God three hundred years, and had sons and daughters. . . .

And Enoch walked with God; and he was not, for God took him. (Genesis 5:22, 24)

4. Noah, His Wife, His Sons, and Their Wives

This is the genealogy of Noah. Noah was a just man, perfect in his generations. Noah walked with God. (Genesis 6:9)

So those that entered, male and female of all flesh, went in as God had commanded him; and the LORD shut him in. (Genesis 7:16)

5. Abraham

Then the LORD appeared to Abram and said, "To your descendants I will give this land." And there he built an altar to the LORD, who had appeared to him. (Genesis 12:7)

So the LORD went His way as soon as He had finished speaking with Abraham; and Abraham returned to his place. (Genesis 18:33)

6. Sarah

Therefore Sarah laughed within herself, saying, "After I have grown old, shall I have pleasure, my lord being old also?" But Sarah denied it, saying, "I did not laugh," for she was afraid. And He said, "No, but you did laugh!" (Genesis 18:12, 15)

And the LORD visited Sarah as He had said, and the LORD did for Sarah as He had spoken. (Genesis 21:1)

7. Hagar

Then she called the name of the LORD who spoke to her, You-Are-the-God-Who-Sees; for she said, "Have I also here seen Him who sees me?" (Genesis 16:13)

8. Ishmael

So God was with the lad [the son of Hagar]. (Genesis 21:20)

9. Isaac

And the LORD appeared to him [Isaac] the same night and said, "I am the God of Abraham your father; fear not, for I am with you and will bless you and multiply your descendants for my servant Abraham's sake." (Genesis 26:24)

10. Rebekah

So she went to inquire of the LORD. And the LORD said to her . . . (Genesis 25:22b–23)

11. *Jacob*

And behold, the LORD stood above it and said: "I am the LORD God of Abraham your father and the God of Isaac; the land on which you lie I will give to you and your descendants. . . . Behold, I am with you and will keep you wherever you go, and will bring you back to this land; for I will not leave you until I have done what I have spoken to you." (Genesis 28:13, 15)

Then God said to Jacob, "Arise, go up to Bethel and dwell there; and make an altar there to God, who appeared to you when you fled from the face of Esau your brother." (Genesis 35:1)

12. *Joseph*

The LORD was with Joseph, and he was a successful man. . . . But the LORD was with Joseph and showed him mercy, and He gave him favor in the sight of the keeper of the prison. (Genesis 39:2a, 21)

And the patriarchs, becoming envious, sold Joseph into Egypt. But God was with him. (Acts 7:9)

13. *Moses*

By faith he [Moses] forsook Egypt, not fearing the wrath of the king; for he endured as seeing Him who is invisible. (Hebrews 11:27)

14. Aaron

Then Moses and Aaron went from the presence of the assembly to the door of the tent of meeting, and fell on their faces. And the glory of the LORD appeared to them. (Numbers 20:6)

15. The Whole Hebrew Congregation

[God told Moses to tell the Israelites] "For today the LORD will appear to you." . . . Then Moses said, "This is the thing which the LORD commanded you to do, and the glory of the LORD will appear to you." (Leviticus 9:4, 6)

And the LORD appeared in the tent in a pillar of cloud; and the pillar of cloud stood by the door of the tent. (Deuteronomy 31:15)

16. Moses and Aaron, Nadab, and Abihu, and Seventy of the Elders of Israel

Then Moses went up, also Aaron, Nadab, and Abihu, and seventy of the elders of Israel, and they saw the God of Israel. . . . But on the nobles of the children of Israel He did not lay His hand. So they saw God, and they ate and drank. (Exodus 24:9–11)

17. Joshua

So the LORD spoke to Moses face to face, as a man speaks to his friend. And he would return to the camp, but his servant Joshua the son of Nun, a young man, did not depart from the tabernacle. (Exodus 33:11)

Then the LORD said to Moses, "Behold, the days approach when you must die; call Joshua, and present yourselves in the tabernacle of meeting, that I may inaugurate him." So Moses and Joshua went and presented themselves in the tabernacle of meeting. . . . Then He inaugurated Joshua the son of Nun, and said, "Be strong and of good courage; for you shall bring the children of Israel into the land of which I swore to them, and I will be with you." (Deuteronomy 31:14, 23)

18. Balaam

The utterance of him who hears the words of God, who sees the vision of the Almighty, who falls down, with eyes wide open. . . . The utterance of him who hears the words of God, and has the knowledge of the Most High, who sees the vision of the Almighty, who falls down, with eyes wide open. (Numbers 24:4, 16)

19. Gideon

And the angel of the LORD appeared to him and said to him, "The LORD is with you, you mighty man of valor." (Judges 6:12)

20. Manoah and His Wife (Samson's Parents)

And the Angel of the LORD appeared to the woman [Manoah's wife, Samson's mother] and said to her, "Indeed now, you are barren and have borne no children; but you shall conceive and bear a son." . . . Then the woman ran in haste and told her husband, and said to him, "Behold, the Man who came to me the *other* day has just now appeared to me!" . . . When the angel of the LORD appeared no more to Manoah and to his wife, then Manoah knew that He *was* the Angel of the LORD. (Judges 13:3, 10, 21)

21. Samuel

But Hannah did not go up, for she said to her husband, "As soon as the child is weaned, I will bring him, that he may appear in the presence of the LORD, and abide there for ever." (1 Samuel 1:22)

And the LORD visited Hannah, and she conceived and bore three sons and two daughters. And the boy Samuel grew in the presence of the LORD. (1 Samuel 2:21)

And the LORD appeared again at Shiloh, for the LORD revealed himself to Samuel at Shiloh by the word of the LORD. (1 Samuel 3:21)

22. David

For David says concerning Him: "I foresaw the LORD always before my face, for He is at my right hand, that I may not be shaken. Therefore my heart rejoiced, and my tongue was glad; moreover my flesh also will rest in hope." (Acts 2:25–26)

I have set the LORD always before me; because He is at my right hand I shall not be moved. . . . You will show me the path of life; in Your presence is fullness of joy; at Your right hand are pleasures forevermore. (Psalm 16:8, 11)

23. Solomon

And the LORD was angry with Solomon, because his heart had turned away from the LORD, the God of Israel, who had appeared to him twice. (1 Kings 11:9)

24. Job

I have heard of You by the hearing of the ear, but now my eye sees You. (Job 42:5)

25. Isaiah

In the year that King Uzziah died, I saw the Lord sitting on a throne, high and lifted up, and the train of His robe filled the temple. (Isaiah 6:1)

26. Micaiah

Then Micaiah said, "Therefore hear the word of the LORD: I saw the LORD sitting on His throne, and all the host of heaven standing on His right hand and His left. (2 Chronicles 18:18)

27. Jeremiah

Moreover the word of the LORD came to me, saying, "Jeremiah, what do you see?" And I said, "I see a branch of an almond tree." Then the LORD said to me, "You have seen well, for I am ready to perform My word." (Jeremiah 1:11–12)

28. Ezekiel

Then I looked, and there was a likeness, like the appearance of fire—from the appearance of His waist and downward, fire; and from His waist and upward, like the appearance of brightness, like the color of amber. . . . And behold, the glory of the God of Israel *was* there, like the vision that I saw in the plain. (Ezekiel 8:2, 4)

29. Nebuchadnezzar, His Counselors, and Shadrach, Meshach, and Abed-Nego

He answered and said, Lo, I see four men loose, walking in the midst of the fire, and they have no hurt; and the form of the fourth is like the Son of God. (Daniel 3:25, KJV)

30. Belshazzar and the Company of One Thousand Lords at the Feast

In the same hour the fingers of a man's hand appeared and wrote opposite the lampstand on the plaster of the wall of the king's palace; and the king saw the part of the hand that wrote. (Daniel 5:5)

31. Daniel

I was watching in the night visions, and behold, One like the Son of Man, coming with the clouds of heaven! He came to the Ancient of Days, and they brought Him near before Him. (Daniel 7:13)

32. Amos

I saw the Lord standing by the altar, and He said: "Strike the doorposts, that the thresholds may shake, and break them on the heads of them all. I will slay the last of them with the sword. He who flees from them shall not get away, and he who escapes from them shall not be delivered." (Amos 9:1)

33. Jonah

But Jonah arose to flee to Tarshish from the presence of the Lord. He went down to Joppa, and found a ship going to Tarshish; so he paid the fare, and went down into it, to go with them to Tarshish from the presence of the Lord. (Jonah 1:3)

34. Habakkuk

God came from Teman, the Holy One from Mount Paran. Selah. His glory covered the heavens, and the earth was full of His praise. (Habakkuk 3:3)

35. Zechariah

And the man who stood among the myrtle trees answered and said, "These are the ones whom the Lord has sent to walk to and fro throughout the earth." So they answered the Angel of the Lord, who stood among the myrtle trees, and said, "We have walked to and fro throughout the earth, and behold, all the earth is resting quietly." Then the Angel of the Lord answered and said,

"O LORD of hosts, how long will You not have mercy on Jerusalem and on the cities of Judah, against which You were angry these seventy years?" And the LORD answered the angel who talked to me, with good and comforting words. (Zechariah 1:10–13)

36. Elijah

Then Elijah said, "As the LORD of hosts lives, before whom I stand, I will surely present myself to him today." (1 Kings 18:15)

37. Elisha

And Elisha said, "As the LORD of hosts lives, before whom I stand, surely were it not that I regard the presence of Jehoshaphat king of Judah, I would not look at you, nor see you." (2 Kings 3:14)

People in the New Testament Who Saw God

1. Jesus Saw God

Then Jesus answered and said to them, "Most assuredly, I say to you, the Son can do nothing of Himself, but what He sees the Father do; for whatever He does, the Son also does in like manner." (John 5:19)

I speak what I have seen with My Father, and you do what you have seen with your father. (John 8:38)

2. All the People Who Saw Jesus in His Earthly Appearance Saw God

[Jesus said] "if you had known Me, you would have known My Father also; and from now on you know Him and have seen Him." . . . Jesus said to him, "Have I been with you so long, and yet you have not known Me, Philip? He who has seen Me has seen the Father; so how can you say, 'Show us the Father'?" (John 14:7, 9)

3. People Who Saw Him in the Physical and Recognized Him as Messiah

a. Mary, Jesus' Mother

And the angel answered and said to her, "[The] Holy Spirit will come upon you, and the power of the Highest will overshadow you; therefore, also, that Holy One who is to be born will be called the Son of God. . . . For with God nothing will be impossible." Then Mary said, "Behold the maidservant of the Lord! Let it be to me according to your word." And the angel departed from her. (Luke 1:35, 37–38)

b. Joseph, Jesus' Earthly Father

Then Joseph her husband, being a just man, and not wanting to make her a public example, was minded to put her away secretly. But while he thought about these things, behold, an angel of the Lord appeared to him in a dream, saying, "Joseph, son of David, do not be afraid to take to you Mary your wife, for that which is conceived in her is of the Holy Spirit. And she will bring forth a Son, and you shall call His name Jesus, for He will save His people from their sins. . . . Then Joseph, being aroused from sleep, did as the angel of the Lord commanded him and took to him his wife, and did not know her till she had brought forth her firstborn Son. And he called His name Jesus. (Matthew 1:19–21, 24–25)

c. Elizabeth

Then she spoke out with a loud voice and said, "Blessed are you among women, and blessed is the fruit of your womb! But why is this granted to me, that the mother of my Lord should come to me." (Luke 1:42–43)

d. Shepherds

Then the shepherds returned, glorifying and praising God for all the things that they had heard and seen, as it was told them. (Luke 2:20)

e. Magi, Wise Men from the East

Wise men from the East came to Jerusalem, saying, "Where is He who has been born King of the Jews? For we have seen His star in the East and have come to worship Him." . . . And when they had come into the house, they saw the young Child with Mary His mother, and fell down and worshiped Him. And when they had opened their treasures, they presented gifts to Him: gold, frankincense, and myrrh. (Matthew 2:1–2, 11)

f. Simeon

And behold, there was a man in Jerusalem whose name was Simeon, and this man was just and devout, waiting for the Consolation of Israel, and the Holy Spirit was upon him. And it had been revealed to him by the Holy Spirit that he would not see death before he had seen the Lord's Christ. So he came by the Spirit into the temple. And when the parents brought in the Child Jesus, to do for Him according to the custom of the law, he took Him up in his arms and blessed God and said: "Lord, now You are letting Your servant depart in peace, according to Your word; for my eyes have seen Your salvation which You have prepared before the face of all peoples, a light to bring revelation to the Gentiles, and the glory of Your people Israel." (Luke 2:25–32)

g. Anna

Anna, a prophetess, was a widow of about eighty-four years, who did not depart from the temple, but served God with fastings and prayers night and day. And coming in that instant she gave thanks to the Lord, and spoke of Him [Jesus] to all those who looked for redemption in Jerusalem. (Luke 2:37–38)

h. John the Baptist

And looking at Jesus as He walked, he said, "Behold the Lamb of God!" (John 1:36)

i. Andrew

He first found his own brother Simon, and said to him, "We have found the Messiah" (which is translated, the Christ). (John 1:41)

j. Peter

Simon Peter answered and said, "You are the Christ, the Son of the living God." (Matthew 16:16)

k. The Woman at the Well

The woman said to Him, "I know that Messiah is coming" (who is called Christ). "When He comes, He will tell us all things." Jesus said to her, "I who speak to you am He."

"Come, see a Man who told me all things that I ever did. Could this be the Christ?" (John 4: 25–26, 29)

l. Martha

She said to Him, "Yes, Lord, I believe that You are the Christ, the Son of God, who is to come into the world." (John 11:27)

m. Mary

Then, when Mary came where Jesus was, and saw Him, she fell down at His feet, saying to Him, "Lord, if You had been here, my brother would not have died." (John 11:42)

n. The Thief on the Cross

Then he said to Jesus, "Lord, remember me when You come into Your kingdom." (Luke 23:42)

o. The Centurion at the Cross

So when the centurion and those with him, who were guarding Jesus, saw the earthquake and the things that had happened, they feared greatly, saying, "Truly this was the Son of God!" (Matthew 27:54)

4. All the Disciples Saw God

That which was from the beginning, which we have heard, which we have seen with our eyes, which we have looked upon, and our hands have handled, concerning the Word of life— (1 John 1:1)

Therefore, of these men who have accompanied us all the time that the Lord Jesus went in and out among us. (Acts 1:21)

5. Peter, James, and John Saw God

He was transfigured before them. . . . And Elijah appeared to them with Moses, and they were talking with Jesus. (Mark 9:2b, 4)

Now there was leaning on Jesus' bosom one of His disciples, whom Jesus loved. (John 13:23)

6. Followers Saw God in Post-Resurrection Appearances

To whom [the apostles] He also presented Himself alive after His suffering by many infallible proofs, being seen by them during forty days and speaking of the things pertaining to the kingdom of God. (Acts 1:3)

And for many days he appeared to those who came up with him from Galilee to Jerusalem, who are now his witnesses to the people. (Acts 13:31)

And . . . He was seen by Cephas, then by the twelve. After that He was seen by over five hundred brethren at once, of whom the greater part remain to the present, but some have fallen asleep. After that He was seen by James, then by all the apostles. Then last of all He was seen by me [Paul] also, as by one born out of due time. (1 Corinthians 15:5–8)

a. Mary Magdalene and Mary

Now after the Sabbath, as the first day of the week began to dawn, Mary Magdalene and the other Mary came to see the tomb. . . . [The Angel said,] "Go quickly and tell His disciples that He is risen from the dead, and indeed He is going before you into Galilee; there you will see Him. Behold, I have told you." . . . And as they went to tell His disciples, behold, Jesus met them, saying, "Rejoice!" So they came and held Him by the feet and worshiped Him. (Matthew 28:1, 7, 9)

Now when He rose early on the first day of the week, He appeared first to Mary Magdalene, out of whom He had cast seven demons. . . . After that, He appeared in another form to two of them as they walked and went into the country. . . . Later He appeared to the eleven as they sat at the table; and He rebuked their unbelief and hardness of heart, because they did not believe those who had seen Him after He had risen. (Mark 16:9, 12, 14)

Mary Magdalene came and told the disciples that she had seen the Lord, and that He had spoken these things to her. (John 20:18)

b. Eleven Disciples

Then the eleven disciples went away into Galilee, to the mountain which Jesus had appointed for them. When they saw Him, they worshiped Him; but some doubted. (Matthew 28:16-17)

And after eight days His disciples were again inside, and Thomas with them. Jesus came, the doors being shut, and stood in the midst, and said, "Peace to you!" (John 20:26)

Simon Peter, Thomas called the Twin, Nathanael of Cana in Galilee, the sons of Zebedee, and two others of His disciples were together. . . . Therefore that disciple whom Jesus loved said to Peter, "It is the Lord!" . . . This is now the third time Jesus showed Himself to His disciples after He was raised from the dead. (John 21:2, 7a, 14)

c. Two Traveling to Emmaus

Now behold, two of them were traveling that same day to a village called Emmaus, which was seven miles from Jerusalem. . . . So it was, while they conversed and reasoned, that Jesus Himself drew near and went with them. But their eyes were restrained, so that they did not know Him. . . . Then their eyes were opened and they knew Him; and He vanished from their sight. (Luke 24:13, 15–16, 31)

d. Five Hundred at His Ascension

Now when He had spoken these things, while they watched, He was taken up, and a cloud received Him out of their sight. And while they looked steadfastly toward heaven as He went up, behold, two men stood by them in white apparel. . . . "This same Jesus, who was taken up from you into heaven, will so come in like manner as you saw Him go into heaven." (Acts 1:9–11b)

7. Post-Ascension Appearances

a. Steven

And said, "Look! I [Steven] see the heavens opened and the Son of Man standing at the right hand of God!" (Acts 7:56)

b. Paul

"But rise and stand on your feet; for I [Jesus] have appeared to you for this purpose, to make you a minister and a witness both of the things which you have seen and of the things which I will yet reveal to you." (Acts 26:16)

I know a man in Christ who fourteen years ago—whether in the body I do not know, or whether out of the body I do not know, God knows—such a one was caught up to the third heaven. (2 Corinthians 12:2)

But I make known to you, brethren, that the gospel which was preached by me is not according to man. For I neither received it from man, nor was I taught it, but it came through the revelation of Jesus Christ. (Galatians 1:11–12)

b. Paul (continued)

Then after fourteen years I went up again to Jerusalem with Barnabas, and also took Titus with me. And I went up by revelation. (Galatians 2:1–2)

c. Ananias

Now there was a certain disciple at Damascus named Ananias; and to him the Lord said in a vision, "Ananias." And he said, "Here I am, Lord." (Acts 9:10)

d. John

Then I turned to see the voice that spoke with me. And having turned I saw seven golden lampstands, and in the midst of the seven lampstands One like the Son of Man, clothed with a garment down to the feet and girded about the chest with a golden band. . . . And when I saw Him, I fell at His feet as dead. But He laid His right hand on me, saying to me, "Do not be afraid; I am the First and the Last." (Revelation 1:12–13, 17)

The World, Including Israel, Will See God at the End of Time

Then the sign of the Son of Man will appear in heaven, and then all the tribes of the earth will mourn, and they will see the Son of Man coming on the clouds of heaven with power and great glory. (Matthew 24:30)

For the LORD shall build up Zion; He shall appear in His glory. (Psalm 102:16)

When Christ who is our life appears, then you also will appear with Him in glory. (Colossians 3:4)

So Christ was offered once to bear the sins of many. To those who eagerly wait for Him He will appear a second time, apart from sin, for salvation. (Hebrews 9:28)

Then the LORD will be seen over them, and His arrow will go forth like lightning. The Lord GOD will blow the trumpet, and go with whirlwinds from the south. (Zechariah 9:14)

Behold, He is coming with clouds, and every eye will see Him, even they who pierced Him. And all the tribes of the earth will mourn because of Him. Even so, Amen. (Revelation 1:7)

But truly, as I live, all the earth shall be filled with the glory of the LORD. (Numbers 14:21)

For I know that my Redeemer lives, And He shall stand at last on the earth; and after my skin is destroyed, this I know, that in my flesh I shall see God, Whom I shall see for myself, and my eyes shall behold, and not another. How my heart yearns within me! (Job 19:25–27)

APPENDIX 5: PEOPLE WHO SAW GOD

Notes

,

Notes

God Can Appear in Different Forms

I think we all agree that angels can appear looking like human beings. "Do not forget to entertain strangers, for by so doing some have unwittingly entertained angels" (Hebrews 13:2). So the question comes, "Does God appear in various forms?" I'm not asking if he, for instance, *is* a tree but can He appear *as* a tree?

> After that, He appeared *in another form* to two of them as they walked and went into the country. (Mark 16:12)

> Now when she [Mary Magdalene] had said this, she turned around and saw Jesus standing there, and *did not know that it was Jesus.* (John 20:14)

Here are some ways God chooses to appear in Scripture.

I. As the Angel of the Lord

A. To Hagar

> Then the *Angel of the LORD* said to her, "I will multiply your descendants exceedingly, so that they shall not be counted for multitude." (Genesis 16:10)

Also see Genesis 21:17.

B. To Jacob

Then the *Angel of God* spoke to me [Jacob] in a dream, saying, "Jacob." And I said, "Here I am." (Genesis 31:11)

C. To Moses

And the *Angel of the* LORD appeared to him [Moses] in a flame of fire from the midst of a bush. So he looked, and behold, the bush was burning with fire, but the bush was not consumed. (Exodus 3:2)

D. To the Camp of Israel

And the *Angel of God*, who went before the camp of Israel, moved and went behind them; and the pillar of cloud went from before them and stood behind them. (Exodus 14:19)

E. Other Examples

1. Balaam and the Donkey (Numbers 22:22–27, 31–35)

2. All the Children of Israel (Judges 2:1, 4)

3. Gideon (Judges 6:11–12, 20–22)

4. Manoah and His Wife (Judges 13:3, 6, 9, 13, 15–18, 20–21)

5. Zechariah (Zechariah 1:11–12; 3:1, 5–6; 12:8)

A tip that the being identified as the Angel of the Lord is indeed God, is that he accepts worship. All other angels refuse to be worshipped in deference to Almighty God.

> Now I, John, saw and heard these things. And when I heard and saw, I fell down to worship before the feet of the angel who showed me these things. Then he said to me, "See *that you do* not *do that.* For I am your fellow servant, and of your brethren the prophets, and of those who keep the words of this book. Worship God. (Revelation 22:8–9)

> The devil said, "Therefore, if You will worship before me, all will be Yours." And Jesus answered and said to him, "Get behind Me, Satan! For it is written, 'You shall worship the LORD your God, and Him only you shall serve.'" (Luke 4:7–8)

II. As a Man

A. *Jesus*

> Let this mind be in you which was also in Christ Jesus, who, being in the form of God, did not consider it robbery to be equal with God, but made Himself of no reputation, taking the form of a bondservant, and coming in the likeness of men. And being found in appearance as a man, He humbled Himself and became obedient to the point of death, even the death of the cross. (Philippians 2:5–8)

127

B. One of the Three Men Who Appeared to Abraham before the Destruction of Sodom

Then the LORD appeared to him by the terebinth trees of Mamre, as he was sitting in the tent door in the heat of the day. So he lifted his eyes and looked, and behold, three men were standing by him; and when he saw them, he ran from the tent door to meet them, and bowed himself to the ground. (Genesis 18:1–2)

C. Wrestling Man

Then Jacob was left alone; and a Man wrestled with him until the breaking of day. (Genesis 32:24)

D. Melchizedek

For this Melchizedek, king of Salem, priest of the Most High God, who met Abraham returning from the slaughter of the kings and blessed him, to whom also Abraham gave a tenth part of all, first being translated "king of righteousness," and then also king of Salem, meaning "king of peace," without father, without mother, without genealogy, having neither beginning of days nor end of life, but made like the Son of God, remains a priest continually. (Hebrews 7:1–3)

See also Genesis 14:18; Psalm 110:4; Hebrews 5:6, 10; 6:20; 7:10–11, 15, 17, 21.

E. Commander of the Army of the Lord

And it came to pass, when Joshua was by Jericho, that he lifted his eyes and looked, and behold, a Man stood opposite him with His sword drawn in His hand. And Joshua went to Him and said to Him, "*Are* You for us or for our adversaries?" So He said, "No, but *as Commander of the army of the LORD* I have now come." And Joshua fell on his face to the earth and worshiped, and said to Him, "What does my Lord say to His servant?" Then the Commander of the LORD's army said to Joshua, "Take your sandal off your foot, for the place where you stand *is* holy." And Joshua did so. (Joshua 5:13–15)

III. As Sound from Heaven, a Rushing Wind, and Fire

And suddenly there came a sound from heaven, as of a rushing mighty wind, and it filled the whole house where they were sitting. Then there appeared to them divided tongues, as of fire, and one sat upon each of them. (Acts 2:2–3)

IV. As a Dove

And when Jesus was baptized, he went up immediately from the water, and behold, the heavens were opened and he saw the Spirit of God descending like a *dove*, and alighting on him. (Matthew 3:16)

And when he came up out of the water, immediately he saw the heavens opened and the Spirit descending upon him like a *dove*. (Mark 1:10)

And the Holy Spirit descended upon him in bodily form, as a *dove*, and a voice came from heaven, "Thou art my beloved Son; with thee I am well pleased." (Luke 3:22)

And John bore witness, "I saw the Spirit descend as a *dove* from heaven, and it remained on him." (John 1:32)

V. As Parts of Himself

Then I will take away My hand, and you shall see My back; but My face shall not be seen. (Exodus 33:23)

In the same hour the fingers of a man's hand appeared and wrote opposite the lampstand on the plaster of the wall of the king's palace; and the king saw the part of the hand that wrote. (Daniel 5:5)

Then the LORD delivered to me two tablets of stone written with the finger of God, and on them were all the words which the LORD had spoken to you on the mountain from the midst of the fire in the day of the assembly. (Deuteronomy 9:10)

VI. As a Lion or a Lamb

But one of the elders said to me, "Do not weep. Behold, the *Lion of the tribe of Judah*, the Root of David, has prevailed to open the scroll and to loose its seven seals." . . . Now when He had taken the scroll, the four living creatures and the twenty-four elders fell down before the *Lamb*, each having a harp, and golden bowls full of incense, which are the prayers of the saints, . . . saying with a loud voice, "Worthy is the *Lamb* who was slain to receive power and wealth and wisdom, and strength and honor and glory and blessing!" And every creature which is in heaven and on the earth and such as are under the earth and in the sea, and all that are in them, I heard saying, "Blessing and honor and glory and power be to Him who sits on the throne, and to the Lamb, forever and ever!" (Revelation 5:5, 8, 12–13)

See also Revelation 6:1, 16; 7:9–10, 14; 12:11; 13:8; 14:1, 4, 10; 15:3; 17:14; 19:7, 9; 21:9, 14, 22–23, 27; 22:1, 3.

VII. As a Ghost

And when the disciples saw Him walking on the sea, they were troubled, saying, "It is a ghost!" And they cried out for fear. But immediately Jesus spoke to them, saying, "Be of good cheer! It is I; do not be afraid." And Peter answered Him and said, "Lord, if it is You, command me to come to You on the water." (Matthew 14:26-28)

See also Mark 6:49.

VIII. As the Word of the Lord

In the beginning was *the Word*, and *the Word* was with God, and *the Word was God*. (John 1:1)

And *the Word* became flesh and dwelt among us, full of grace and truth; we have beheld his glory, glory as of the only Son from the Father. (John 1:14)

For the *word of the LORD* is upright; and all his work is done in faithfulness. (Psalm 33:4)

By the *word of the LORD* the heavens were made, and all their host by the breath of his mouth. (Psalm 33:6)

He was clothed with a robe dipped in blood, and His name is called *The Word of God*. (Revelation 19:13)

A. Abram

After these things the *word of the LORD* came to Abram in a vision, "Do not be afraid, Abram. I am your shield, your exceedingly great reward." . . . And behold, the word of the LORD came to him, saying, "This one shall not be your heir, but one who will come from your own body shall be your heir." . . . Then He said to him, "I am the LORD." (Genesis 15:1, 4, 7)

B. Samuel

Now the boy Samuel was ministering to the LORD under Eli. And the *word of the LORD* was rare in those days; there was no frequent vision. (1 Samuel 3:1)

Now Samuel did not yet know the LORD, and the *word of the LORD* had not yet been revealed to him. (1 Samuel 3:7)

And the LORD appeared again at Shiloh, for the LORD revealed himself to Samuel at Shiloh by the *word of the LORD.* (1 Samuel 3:21)

The *word of the LORD* came to Samuel. (1 Samuel 15:10)

C. Others to Whom the Word Appeared

1. Nathan (2 Samuel 7:4; 12:9; 1 Chronicles 17:3)

2. Gad (2 Samuel 24:11)

3. Solomon (1 Kings 6:11)

4. Jehu (1 Kings 16:1, 7)

5. Elijah (1 Kings 17:2, 8; 18:1; 19:9; 21:17, 28)

6. Jacob (1 Kings 18:31)

7. Isaiah (2 Kings 20:4; Isaiah 38:4)

8. David (1 Chronicles 22:8)

9. Shemaiah, the Man of God (2 Chronicles 11:2; 2:7)

10. Joseph (Psalm 105:19)

11. Jeremiah (Jeremiah 1:2, 4, 11, 13; 2:1; 13:3, 8; 14:1; 16:1; 18:5; 24:4; 28:12; 29:30; 32:6, 26; 33:1, 19, 23; 34:12; 35:12; 36:27; 37:6; 39:15; 42:7; 43:8; 46:1; 47:1; 49:34)

12. Ezekiel (Ezekiel 1:3; 3:16; 6:1; 7:1; 11:14; 12:8, 17; 12:21, 26; 13:1; 14:2, 12; 15:1; 16:1; 17:1, 11; 18:1; 20:2, 45; 21:1, 8, 18; 22:1, 17, 23; 23:1; 24:1,15, 20; 25:1; 26:1; 27:1; 28:1, 11, 20; 29:1, 17; 30:1, 20; 31:1; 32:1, 17; 33:1, 23; 34:1, 7, 9; 35:1; 36:1, 4; 36:16; 37:4, 15; 38:1)

13. Hosea (Hosea 1:1)

14. Joel (Joel 1:1)

15. Jonah (Jonah 1:1)

16. Micah (Micah 1:1)

17. Zephaniah (Zephaniah 1:1)

18. Haggai (Haggai 1:1–3; 2:1, 10, 20)

19. Zechariah (Zechariah 1:1, 7; 4:8; 6:9; 7:1, 4, 8; 8:1, 18; 9:1; 11:11; 12:1)

20. Peter (Acts 11:16)

IX. As the Lampstand

And he said to me, "What do you see?" So I said, "I am looking, and there is a lampstand of solid gold with a bowl on top of it, and on the stand seven lamps with seven pipes to the seven lamps. Two olive trees are by it, one at the right of the bowl and the other at its left." . . . So he said, "These are the two anointed ones, who stand beside the Lord of the whole earth." (Zechariah 4:2–3, 14)

And in the midst of the seven lampstands One like the Son of Man, clothed with a garment down to the feet and girded about the chest with a golden band. (Revelation 1:13)

Remember therefore from where you have fallen; repent and do the first works, or else I will come to you quickly and remove your lampstand from its place—unless you repent. (Revelation 2:5)

And from the throne proceeded lightnings, thunderings, and voices. Seven lamps of fire were burning before the throne, which are the seven Spirits of God. (Revelation 4:5)

X. As a Smoking Oven and a Burning Torch

And it came to pass, when the sun went down and it was dark, that behold, there appeared a smoking oven and a burning torch that passed between those pieces. (Genesis 15:17)

XI. God Also Seems to Use Signs of His Presence

A. A Pillar of Fire and a Cloud

And the LORD went before them by day in a pillar of cloud to lead them along the way, and by night in a *pillar of fire* to give them light, that they might travel by day and by night. (Exodus 13:21)

Now it came to pass, in the morning watch, that the LORD looked down upon the army of the Egyptians through the *pillar of fire and cloud*, and He troubled the army of the Egyptians. (Exodus 14:24)

And they will tell *it* to the inhabitants of this land. They have heard that You, LORD, *are* among these people; that You, LORD, are seen face to face and Your cloud stands above them, and You go before them in a *pillar of cloud* by day and in a *pillar of fire* by night. (Numbers 14:14)

Also see Nehemiah 9:12, 19.

B. A Whirlwind

And behold, the LORD passed by, and a great and strong wind tore into the mountains and broke the rocks in pieces before the LORD, but the LORD was not in the wind; and after the wind an earthquake, but the LORD was not in the earthquake; and after the earthquake a fire, but the

LORD was not in the fire; and after the fire a still small voice. (1 Kings 19:11–12)

Then the LORD answered Job out of the *whirlwind*. (Job 38:1)

C. Storms and Natural Phenomena

The voice of the LORD *is* over the waters; the God of glory thunders; the LORD *is* over many waters. (Psalm 29:3)

Then the temple of God was opened in heaven, and the ark of His covenant was seen in His temple. And there were lightnings, noises, thunderings, an earthquake, and great hail. (Revelation 11:19)

D. A Burning Bush

And *the Angel of the* LORD appeared to him [Moses] in a flame of fire from the midst of a bush. So he looked, and behold, the bush was burning with fire, but the bush was not consumed. (Exodus 3:2)

E. A Rock

And what do we do with *the Rock*? Was it metaphorical or was it a visible sign of his presence?

E. A Rock (cont.)

The God of Israel said, the Rock of Israel spoke to me: "He who rules over men must be just, ruling in the fear of God." (2 Samuel 23:3)

Are You not from everlasting, O Lord my God, my Holy One? We shall not die. O Lord, You have appointed them for judgment; O Rock, You have marked them for correction. (Habakkuk 1:12)

And all drank the same spiritual drink. For they drank of that spiritual Rock that followed them, and that Rock was Christ. (1 Corinthians 10:4)

XII. And Finally, in the Mystical Forms of His Glory

A. Jesus Transfigured

And He was transfigured before them. His face shone like the sun, and His clothes became as white as the light. (Matthew 17:2)

B. Daniel's Vision of the Ancient of Days and One Like the Son of Man

I watched till thrones were put in place, and the Ancient of Days *was* seated; His garment *was* white as snow, and the hair of His head *was* like pure wool. His throne *was* a fiery flame, its wheels a burning fire. . . . I was watching in the night visions, and behold, *One* like the Son of Man, coming with the clouds of heaven! He came to the Ancient of Days, and they brought Him near before Him. . . . The Ancient of Days came, and a judgment was made *in favor* of the saints of the Most High, and the time came for the saints to possess the kingdom. (Daniel 7:9, 13, 22)

C. Ezekiel's Visions

And above the firmament over their heads *was* the likeness of a throne, in appearance like a sapphire stone; on the likeness of the throne *was* a likeness with the appearance of a man high above it. Also from the appearance of His waist and upward I saw, as it were, the color of amber with the appearance of fire all around within it; and from the appearance of His waist and downward I saw, as it were, the appearance of fire with brightness all around. Like the appearance of a rainbow in a cloud on a rainy day, so *was* the appearance of the brightness all around it. This *was* the appearance of the likeness of the glory of the LORD. So when I saw *it*, I fell on my face, and I heard a voice of One speaking. (Ezekiel 1:26–28)

D. Zechariah's Visions

I saw by night, and behold, a man riding on a red horse, and it stood among the myrtle trees in the hollow; and

D. Zechariah's Visions (cont.)

behind him *were* horses: red, sorrel, and white. . . . And *the man who stood among the myrtle trees* answered and said, "These *are the ones* whom the LORD has sent to walk to and fro throughout the earth." So they answered the Angel of the LORD, who stood among the myrtle trees, and said, "We have walked to and fro throughout the earth, and behold, all the earth is resting quietly." Then the Angel of the LORD answered and said, "O LORD of hosts, how long will You not have mercy on Jerusalem and on the cities of Judah, against which You were angry these seventy years?" And the LORD answered the angel who talked to me, *with* good *and* comforting words. (Zechariah 1:8, 10–13)

Then he showed me Joshua the high priest standing before the Angel of the LORD, and Satan standing at his right hand to oppose him. And the LORD said to Satan, "The LORD rebuke you, Satan! The LORD who has chosen Jerusalem rebuke you! *Is* this not a brand plucked from the fire?" Now Joshua was clothed with filthy garments, and was standing before the Angel. Then He answered and spoke to those who stood before Him, saying, "Take away the filthy garments from him." And to him He said, "See, I have removed your iniquity from you, and I will clothe you with rich robes." And I said, "Let them put a clean turban on his head." So they put a clean turban on his head, and they put the clothes on him. And the Angel of the LORD stood by. (Zechariah 3:1–5)

E. John's Revelation of Jesus Christ

And in the midst of the seven lampstands *One* like the Son of Man, clothed with a garment down to the feet and girded about the chest with a golden band. His head and hair *were* white like wool, as white as snow, and His eyes like a flame of fire; His feet *were* like fine brass, as if refined in a furnace, and His voice as the sound of many waters; He had in His right hand seven stars, out of His mouth went a sharp two–edged sword, and His countenance *was* like the sun shining in its strength. And when I saw Him, I fell at His feet as dead. But He laid His right hand on me, saying to me, "Do not be afraid; I am the First and the Last. I *am* He who lives, and was dead, and behold, I am alive forevermore. Amen. And I have the keys of Hades and of Death." (Revelation 1:13–18)

Then I looked, and behold, a white cloud, and on the cloud sat *One* like the Son of Man, having on His head a golden crown, and in His hand a sharp sickle. (Revelation 14:14)

Now I saw heaven opened, and behold, a white horse. And He who sat on him *was* called Faithful and True, and in righteousness He judges and makes war. His eyes *were* like a flame of fire, and on His head *were* many crowns. He had a name written that no one knew except Himself. He *was* clothed with a robe dipped in blood, and His name is called The Word of God. And the armies in heaven, clothed in fine linen, white and clean, followed

E. John's Revelation of Jesus Christ (cont.)

Him on white horses. Now out of His mouth goes a sharp sword, that with it He should strike the nations. And He Himself will rule them with a rod of iron. He Himself treads the winepress of the fierceness and wrath of Almighty God. And He has on *His* robe and on His thigh a name written: KING OF KINGS AND LORD OF LORDS. . . . And I saw the beast, the kings of the earth, and their armies, gathered together to make war against Him who sat on the horse and against His army. . . . And the rest were killed with the sword which proceeded from the mouth of Him who sat on the horse. And all the birds were filled with their flesh. (Revelation 19:11–16, 19, 21)

F. Matthew's Jesus, the Judge of the Nations

When the Son of Man comes in His glory, and all the holy angels with Him, then He will sit on the throne of His glory. All the nations will be gathered before Him, and He will separate them one from another, as a shepherd divides *his* sheep from the goats. (Matthew 25:31–32)

I included this passage because I wonder if Matthew was privileged to see the scene he could describe so vividly.

Notes

Why See?

My husband was drafted five months after we were married. It was at the height of the Vietnam War. My greatest fear was that he would be killed and that my life would be over at twenty-two years of age. I dropped him off at the Columbus bus depot at 6:00 AM hoping against hope that his enlarged spleen, diagnosed as a teenager, would disqualify him from service. By noon, I hadn't heard from him. Later that day, he managed to call to tell me that he had been accepted for service. He didn't know where he was going, and he didn't know when he'd be able to let me know. He loved me, good bye.

Several days later, I received my first letter. Contact. What a joy! Just to hear from him and know that he was still alive. He wrote every day he could, and I lived on those letters. I learned when the postman was likely to arrive and ran to get my letters, which I eagerly read and read again, cherishing each word of information and love. And then I waited hungrily, day after day, for the next installment. But there finally came a day when he was able to call me on the phone across from his barracks. What absolute joy! Just to hear his voice and sense his closeness. He continued to write daily letters as he could and I continued to devour them day by day, but his voice, I longed to hear his voice again. Periodically, he'd be able to call. I was always waiting, but still surprised when his calls came because there was no set time.

I didn't know what to expect. Would I ever see him again, and if so, when? As basic training drew to an end, the answer finally came. Mike called to let me know that he and his unit had weekend passes. He couldn't leave because somebody in his unit had messed up, but I could come down to Georgia and spend the weekend with him on the base. Is there anything beyond joy? Maybe fullness of joy? I got into the car and drove all seventeen hours, through the night, singing at the top of my lungs with the window open (partly to stay awake). But to *see* him and have him enfold me in his arms and to experience him. Yes, I had letters written by him that told me what he was doing and how he was; I had heard his voice and talked with him. But nothing compared to seeing him, experiencing him and the love he had for me.

That's "Why See?". I began with the precious Scriptures, which I cherish and read over and over again because they tell me about Jesus. Then I heard His voice. I loved hearing his voice so much that one day I said to Him, "I don't care if you correct me, teach me, help me with my problems or not, say whatever you want, just let me hear your voice." But when I began seeing Him, experiencing him more fully . . .

Why Not See?

My suggestion is that we all are affected by wounds, lies, and sin that have built barriers and partially blocked our knowledge of God. We are afraid of the intimacy that means experiencing God with the whole spiritual package of seeing, hearing, feeling, smelling, and tasting. We are afraid to make a mistake. We are afraid of offending him, of breaking the law or misreading the Scripture. We are afraid he won't be nice or that he will leave us alone or that he is something other than what Scripture tells us—good and powerful. These "arguments and every high thing that exalts itself against the knowledge of God" (2 Corinthians 10:5) live in our unhealed hearts and cause us to hide from the One who loves us so much.

Why See Since I Can Hear Already?

At one seminar a man was simply staring instead of practicing finding Jesus in the room with his partner. I asked him why he wasn't doing the exercise. "Don't you want to see him?" I said. "Nope, I already hear him just fine." "But don't you want to know him better?" "Nope, I know him well enough!"

I remember when TVs became available. (OK, do the math— I'm old.) None of us said to our parents, "Oh, please don't get us a TV, we only want the radio. I think most of us would rather watch and hear the TV than listen to the radio." By the way, when color TVs became available, we wanted to see better—in color. And how many of us love our HDTV? Do you want to go back? I don't.

Why See If I Can Be More Blessed If I Don't See?

One man thought that when Jesus said to Thomas in John 20:29, "Because you have seen Me, you have believed. Blessed *are* those who have not seen and *yet* have believed" that Jesus meant it would be more spiritual to not see! Jesus was speaking to Thomas's doubt. Even though Thomas walked with Jesus on earth, he was slow to believe.

> Now Thomas, called the Twin, one of the twelve, was not with them when Jesus came. The other disciples therefore said to him, "We have seen the Lord." So he said to them,

"Unless I see in His hands the print of the nails, and put my finger into the print of the nails, and put my hand into His side, I will not believe." And after eight days His disciples were again inside, and Thomas with them. Jesus came, the doors being shut, and stood in the midst, and said, "Peace to you!" Then He said to Thomas, "Reach your finger here, and look at My hands; and reach your hand here, and put it into My side. Do not be unbelieving, but believing." And Thomas answered and said to Him, "My Lord and my God!" (John 20:24–28)

Jesus was comparing Thomas's faith, dependent on seeing and feeling Jesus up close, with the faith of those who believe without personally seeing and feeling him. Jesus wasn't telling us to refuse a blessing by stopping the Holy Spirit from revealing Jesus to us through our visual senses and/or mental imagery.

Why See If I Have a Chance of Being Deceived?

Scripture informs and confirms that we can see in the Spirit.

God corrects those he loves and will let you know if you are off track.

You can never pursue the Lord too much.

Faith pleases God.

He knows your heart.

It's Holy Spirit's job to reveal Jesus.

If you've seen the Son, you've seen the Father.

Jesus confirms his Word.

God is more powerful to reveal truth than the Devil is to deceive.

Why See?

God wants us to know him, And he wants to know us. He describes eternal life in terms of intimacy (John 17:3). He describes his eternal relationship with us as Bridegroom and bride. We are to "Grow in the grace and knowledge of our Lord and Savior Jesus Christ. To Him be the glory both now and forever. Amen" (2 Peter 3:18).

Choose to see.

APPENDIX 7: WHY SEE?

Notes

Notes

Objections to Seeing God

Objection 1: You Can't See God

I. Supportive Scriptures

No one has seen God at any time. The only begotten Son, who is in the bosom of the Father, He has declared *Him*. (John 1:18)

And the Father Himself, who sent Me, has testified of Me. You have neither heard His voice at any time, nor seen His form. (John 5:37)

Who alone has immortality, dwelling in unapproachable light, whom no man has seen or can see, to whom be honor and everlasting power. Amen. (1 Timothy 6:16)

II. Answers to Objection 1

A. People Survived Encountering God

People of the Old Testament believed they would die if they saw him, but they did not die when they encountered him face to face!

She called the name of the LORD who spoke to her, "Thou art a God of seeing"; for she said, "Have I really seen God and remained alive after seeing him?" (Genesis 16:13)

A. People Survived Encountering God (continued)

Jacob called the name of the place Peniel, saying, "For I have seen God face to face, and yet my life is preserved." (Genesis 32:30)

Behold, the LORD our God has shown us his glory and greatness, and we have heard his voice out of the midst of the fire; we have this day seen God speak with man and man still live. (Deuteronomy 5:24)

Manoah said to his wife, "We shall surely die, because we have seen God!" (Judges 13:22)

B. God Accommodates Our Humanity

God tailors his perceived presence for our humanity. All his glory, splendor, majesty, joy, brilliance, dimensionality, brightness, cognition, and other attributes would destroy us.

And he said, "Please, show me Your glory." Then He said, "I will make all My goodness pass before you, and I will proclaim the name of the LORD before you. I will be gracious to whom I will be gracious, and I will have compassion on whom I will have compassion." But He said, "You cannot see My face; for no man shall see Me, and live." And the LORD said, "Here is a place by Me, and you shall stand on the rock. So it shall be, while My glory passes by, that I will put you in the cleft of the rock, and will cover you with My hand while I pass by. Then I will take away My hand, and you shall see My back; but My face shall not be seen." (Exodus 33:18–23)

C. God Reveals Himself to People

Here are some ways he revealed himself to people.

1. Moses and Joshua met God at the tent of meeting before the tabernacle was completed.

So Moses and Aaron went from the presence of the assembly to the door of the tabernacle of meeting, and they fell on their faces. And the glory of the LORD appeared to them. (Numbers 20:6)

So Moses and Joshua went and presented themselves in the tabernacle of meeting. Now the LORD appeared at the tabernacle in a pillar of cloud, and the pillar of cloud stood above the door of the tabernacle. (Deuteronomy 31:14b–15)

2. God's presence was above the ark of the covenant, over the mercy seat, between the cherubim.

a. God's presence was seen and heard there.

You shall put the mercy seat on top of the ark, and in the ark you shall put the Testimony that I will give you. And there I will meet with you, and I will speak with you from above the mercy seat, from between the two cherubim which *are* on the ark of the Testimony. (Exodus 25:21–22a)

So the people sent to Shiloh, that they might bring from thence the ark of the covenant of the LORD of hosts, which dwelleth between the cherubims: and the two sons of Eli, Hophni and Phinehas, were there with the ark of the covenant of God. (1 Samuel 4:4, KJV)

2. God's presence with the ark of the covenant (cont.)

b. God's presence in rested on the ark when the Philistines took the ark to Philistia as a prize of war. See 1 Samuel 4:17, 21; 5:1–12.

So they sent and gathered together all the lords of the Philistines, and said, "Send away the ark of the God of Israel, and let it go back to its own place, so that it does not kill us and our people." For there was a deadly destruction throughout all the city; the hand of God was very heavy there. (1 Samuel 5:11)

c. God's presence was on the ark at Obed-Edom's house.

So David would not move the ark of the LORD with him into the City of David; but David took it aside into the house of Obed–Edom the Gittite. The ark of the LORD remained in the house of Obed–Edom the Gittite three months. And the LORD blessed Obed–Edom and all his household. (2 Samuel 6:10–11)

d. God's unveiled presence was in the tabernacle of David.

Thus all Israel brought up the ark of the covenant of the LORD with shouting and with the sound of the horn, with trumpets and with cymbals, making music with stringed instruments and harps. And it happened, *as* the ark of the covenant of the LORD came to the City of David ... (1 Chronicles 15:28–29)

So they brought the ark of God, and set it in the midst of the tabernacle that David had erected for it. Then they offered burnt offerings and peace offerings before God. . . . And he appointed some of the Levites to minister before the ark of the LORD, to commemorate, to thank, and to praise the LORD God of Israel. . . . Benaiah and Jahaziel the priests regularly *blew* the trumpets before the ark of the covenant of God. . . . So he left Asaph and his brothers there before the ark of the covenant of the LORD to minister before the ark regularly, as every day's work required. (1 Chronicles 16:1, 4, 6, 37)

e. The high priests in the Holy of Holies experienced God in both the tabernacle and the temple.

And the LORD said to Moses: "Tell Aaron your brother not to come at *just* any time into the Holy *Place* inside the veil, before the mercy seat which *is* on the ark, lest he die; for I will appear in the cloud above the mercy seat." (Leviticus 16:2)

We may perform the service of the LORD before Him with our burnt offerings, with our sacrifices, and with our peace offerings; that your descendants may not say to our descendants in time to come, "You have no part in the LORD." (Joshua 22:27)

3. God appeared in Old Testament theophanies (pre-incarnate appearances of Jesus).

a. The Angel of the Lord—See appendix 6, "God Can Appear in Different Forms," under section I.

3. God appeared in Old Testament theophanies (cont.)

b. Melchizedek, King of Peace and High Priest forever is God—
See appendix 6, section II, point D: "God Can Appear in Different Forms."

*c. Commander of the Lord's Army (Captain of the Host)—*See appendix 6, section II, point E, "God Can Appear in Different Forms."

4. Jesus came in the form of a man.

Who [Jesus], being in the form of God, did not consider it robbery to be equal with God, but made Himself of no reputation, taking the form of a bondservant, *and* coming in the likeness of men. And *being found in appearance as a man*, He humbled Himself and became obedient to *the point of* death, even the death of the cross. (Philippians 2:6–8)

D. God Is Both Transcendent and Immanent

"*Am* I a God near at hand," says the LORD, "And not a God afar off?" (Jeremiah 23:23)

Now to Him who is able to keep you from stumbling, and to present *you* faultless before the presence of His glory with exceeding joy, to God our Savior, Who alone is wise, *be* glory and majesty, dominion and power, both now and forever. Amen. (Jude 1:24–25)

Take My yoke upon you and learn from Me, for I am gentle and lowly in heart, and you will find rest for your souls. (Matthew 11:29)

Who being the brightness of *His* glory and the express image of His person, and upholding all things by the word of His power, when He had by Himself purged our sins, sat down at the right hand of the Majesty on high. (Hebrews 1:3)

Therefore God also has highly exalted Him and given Him the name which is above every name, that at the name of Jesus every knee should bow, of those in heaven, and of those on earth, and of those under the earth, and *that* every tongue should confess that Jesus Christ *is* Lord, to the glory of God the Father. (Philippians 2:9–11)

My beloved [Jesus, my interpretation] is like a gazelle or a young stag. Behold, he stands behind our wall; He is looking through the windows, gazing through the lattice. My beloved spoke, and said to me: "Rise up, my love, my fair one, and come away." (Song of Solomon 2:9–10)

Who *is* like You, O LORD, among the gods? Who *is* like You, glorious in holiness, fearful in praises, doing wonders? (Exodus 15:11)

Where were you when I laid the foundations of the earth? Tell *Me*, if you have understanding. . . . Have the gates of death been revealed to you? Or have you seen the doors of the shadow of death? . . . Have you entered the treasury of snow, or have you seen the treasury of hail? . . . Can you bind the cluster of the Pleiades, or loose the belt of Orion? (Job 38:4, 17, 22, 31)

Objection 2: Jesus Is Not Omnipresent; He Is out of Our Sight, Physically Seated at the Right Hand of God

A woman wrote to tell me that she had to repent and ask God's forgiveness for seeing Jesus at one of my seminars. Although she had seen and talked with him, her husband and Christian community confirmed all her doubts and fears when she returned home. They said Jesus is not omnipresent. They believed that since he has a physical body, he can only be in one place at a time. They reason that if He is sitting at the right hand of God, we can't experience him. Didn't he say, "You will see me no more?" she wrote. "Therefore," she warned, "you are on dangerous territory—Extra-Biblical and New Age Territory." She reminded me that blaspheming the Holy Spirit is *unforgiveable*. Unfortunately she didn't ask her questions, but my hope is that the following will help you understand what the Scriptures have to say about it.

I. Supportive Scriptures

Jesus is sitting (a sign that his work is finished) at his rightful place of honor and power at the right hand of the Father in heaven.

So then, after the Lord had spoken to them, He was received up into heaven, and sat down at the right hand of God. (Mark 16:19)

Hereafter the Son of Man will sit on the right hand of the power of God. (Luke 22:69)

It is Christ who died, and furthermore is also risen, who is even at the right hand of God, who also makes intercession for us. (Romans 8:34b)

Who being the brightness of *His* glory and the express image of His person, and upholding all things by the word of His power, . . . sat down at the right hand of the Majesty on high. (Hebrews 1:3)

We have such a High Priest, who is seated at the right hand of the throne of the Majesty in the heavens. (Hebrews 8:1b)

But this Man, after He had offered one sacrifice for sins forever, sat down at the right hand of God. (Hebrews 10:12)

II. Answers to Objection 2

A. Scripture Directs Us to Look to Jesus Who Is Seated at the Right Hand of the Father in Heaven

Looking unto Jesus, the author and finisher of *our* faith, who for the joy that was set before Him endured the cross, despising the shame, and has sat down at the right hand of the throne of God. (Hebrews 12:2)

Stephen is our example.

> But he [Stephen], being full of the Holy Spirit, gazed into heaven and saw the glory of God, and Jesus standing at the right hand of God, and said, "Look! I see the heavens opened and the Son of Man standing at the right hand of God!" (Acts 7:55–56)

B. While Jesus Is Seated at the Right Hand of the Father in Heaven, He Tells Us That We Will See Him There and See Him Coming in the Clouds

> Jesus said to him, "It is as you said. Nevertheless, I say to you, hereafter you will see the Son of Man sitting at the right hand of the Power, and coming on the clouds of heaven." (Matthew 26:64)

> Jesus said, "I am. You will see the Son of Man sitting at the right hand of the Power, and coming with the clouds of heaven." (Mark 14:62)

C. We Are Seated with Him in Heavenly Places

> If then you were raised with Christ, seek those things which are above, where Christ is, sitting at the right hand of God. (Colossians 3:1)

> To him who overcomes I will grant to sit with Me on My throne, as I also overcame and sat down with My Father on His throne. (Revelation 3:21)

And what *is* the exceeding greatness of His power toward us who believe, according to the working of His mighty power, which He worked in Christ when He raised Him from the dead and seated *Him* at His right hand in the heavenly *places*. (Ephesians 1:19–20)

Even when we were dead in trespasses, made us alive together with Christ, (by grace you have been saved), and raised us up together, and made us sit together in the heavenly places in Christ Jesus. (Ephesians 2:5–6)

D. While We Are Seated with Jesus in Heavenly Places Together, He Also Lives in Us by His Spirit

"A little while longer and the world will see Me no more, but you will see Me. Because I live, you will live also. At that day you will know that I *am* in My Father, and you in Me, and I in you. He who has My commandments and keeps them, it is he who loves Me. And he who loves Me will be loved by My Father, and I will love him and manifest Myself to him." Judas (not Iscariot) said to Him, "Lord, how is it that You will manifest Yourself to us, and not to the world?" Jesus answered and said to him, "If anyone loves Me, he will keep My word; and My Father will love him, and We will come to him and make Our home with him." (John 14:19–23)

You are already clean because of the word which I have spoken to you. Abide in Me, and I in you. As the branch cannot bear fruit of itself, unless it abides in the vine,

D. While We Are Seated with Jesus in Heavenly Places Together, He Also Lives in Us by His Spirit (cont.)

neither can you, unless you abide in Me. I am the vine, you *are* the branches. He who abides in Me, and I in him, bears much fruit; for without Me you can do nothing. If anyone does not abide in Me, he is cast out as a branch and is withered; and they gather *them* and throw them into the fire, and they are burned. (John 15:3–6)

I have been crucified with Christ; it is no longer I who live, but Christ lives in me; and the *life* which I now live in the flesh I live by faith in the Son of God, who loved me and gave Himself for me. (Galatians 2:20)

E. It's the Father Who Sends the Spirit of Wisdom and the Spirit of Revelation/Understanding (Holy Spirit) to Reveal Jesus to Us

In this the love of God was manifested toward us, that God has sent His only begotten Son into the world, that we might live through Him. (1 John 4:9)

Do not cease to give thanks for you, making mention of you in my prayers: that the God of our Lord Jesus Christ, the Father of glory, may give to you the spirit of wisdom and revelation in the knowledge of Him.
(Ephesians 1:16–17)

Jesus answered and said to him, "Blessed are you, Simon Bar-Jonah, for flesh and blood has not revealed *this* to you, but My Father who is in heaven." (Matthew 16:17)

But the Helper, the Holy Spirit, whom the Father will send in My name, He will teach you all things, and bring to your remembrance all things that I said to you. (John 14:26)

But as it is written: "Eye has not seen, nor ear heard, nor have entered into the heart of man the things which God has prepared for those who love Him." But God has revealed *them* to us through His Spirit. For the Spirit searches all things, yes, the deep things of God. For what man knows the things of a man except the spirit of the man which is in him? Even so no one knows the things of God except the Spirit of God. (1 Corinthians 2:9–11)

F. Jesus Reveals the Father

Jesus said to him, "Have I been with you so long, and yet you have not known Me, Philip? He who has seen Me has seen the Father; so how can you say, 'Show us the Father'? Do you not believe that I am in the Father, and the Father in Me? The words that I speak to you I do not speak on My own *authority*; but the Father who dwells in Me does the works. Believe Me that I *am* in the Father and the Father in Me, or else believe Me for the sake of the works themselves." (John 14:9–11)

APPENDIX 8: OBJECTIONS TO SEEING GOD

Notes

Notes

God Accepts and Loves Intimacy with Us

God Chose Intimate, Face-to-Face Relationships with People in the Old Testament

Then *Jacob* was left alone; and a Man wrestled with him until the breaking of day. Now when He saw that He did not prevail against him, He touched the socket of his hip; and the socket of Jacob's hip was out of joint as He wrestled with him. . . . So Jacob called the name of the place Peniel: "For I have seen God *face to face*, and my life is preserved." (Genesis 32:24–25, 30)

So the LORD spoke to Moses *face to face*, as a man speaks to his friend. And he would return to the camp, but his servant Joshua the son of Nun, a young man, *did not depart* from the tabernacle. (Exodus 33:11)

And they will tell it to the inhabitants of this land. They have heard that You, LORD, *are* among these people; that You, LORD, are seen *face to face* and Your cloud stands above them, and You go before them in a pillar of cloud by day and in a pillar of fire by night. (Numbers 14:14)

So he [Moses] was there with the LORD forty days and forty nights; he neither ate bread nor drank water. And He wrote on the tablets the words of the covenant, the Ten Commandments. (Exodus 34:28)

The LORD bless you and keep you; the LORD make His face shine upon you, and be gracious to you; the LORD lift up His countenance upon you, and give you peace. (Numbers 6:24–26)

The LORD talked with you *face to face* on the mountain from the midst of the fire. (Deuteronomy 5:4)

Now *Gideon* perceived that He *was* the Angel of the LORD. So Gideon said, "Alas, O Lord GOD! For I have seen the Angel of the LORD *face to face.*" (Judges 6:22)

Seek the LORD and His strength; seek His face evermore! (Psalm 105:4; 1 Chronicles 16:11)

Hear, O LORD, *when* I cry with my voice! Have mercy also upon me, and answer me. *When You said,* "Seek My face," my heart said to You, "*Your face,* LORD, I will seek." Do not hide *Your face* from me; do not turn Your servant away in anger; You have been my help; do not leave me nor forsake me, O God of my salvation. When my father and my mother forsake me, then the LORD will take care of me. (Psalm 27:7–10)

Abraham Is Described as a Friend of God

And the Scripture was fulfilled which says, *"Abraham believed God, and it was accounted to him for righteousness."* And he was called the *friend of God.* (James 2:23)

Then the LORD *appeared* to Abram and said, "To your descendants I will give this land." So he built there an altar to the LORD, who had *appeared* to him. (Genesis 12:7)

When Abram was ninety-nine years old, the Lord appeared to Abram and said to him, "I am God Almighty; walk before Me, and be blameless." . . . Then He finished talking with him, and *God went up* from Abraham. (Genesis 17:1, 22)

Then the LORD *appeared* to him by the terebinth trees of Mamre,as he was sitting in the tent door in the heat of the day. So he lifted his eyes and looked, and behold, three men were standing by him; and when he saw them, he ran from the tent door to meet them, and bowed himself to the ground. . . . And the LORD said, "Shall I hide from Abraham what I am doing? . . . For I have known him." (Genesis 18:1–2, 17, 19a)

[The LORD said,] "*I will go down now and see* whether they have done altogether according to the outcry against it that has come to Me; and if not, I will know." Then the men turned away from there and went toward Sodom, *but Abraham still stood before the LORD. And Abraham came near* and said, "Would You also destroy the righteous with the wicked?" . . . So *the LORD went His way* as soon as He had finished speaking with Abraham. (Genesis 18:21–23, 18:33a)

We Can Be a Friend of God Too

But if anyone loves God, this one is known by Him. (1 Corinthians 8:3)

He who loves purity of heart *and has* grace on his lips, the king *will* be his friend. (Proverbs 22:11)

Blessed are the pure in heart, for they shall see God. (Matthew 5:8)

You are *My friends*, if you do whatever I command you. No longer do I call you servants, for a servant does not know what his master is doing; but I have called you friends, for all things that I heard from My Father I have made known to you. (John 15:14–15)

Those Choosing Not to Know God Will Not Have a Relationship with Him

And he did evil, because he did not prepare his heart to seek the LORD. (2 Chronicles 12:14)

And whoever would not seek the LORD God of Israel was to be put to death, whether small or great, whether man or woman. (2 Chronicles 15:13)

Woe to those who go down to Egypt for help, *and* rely on horses, who trust in chariots because *they* are many, and in horsemen because they are very strong, but who do not look to the Holy One of Israel, nor seek the Lord! (Isaiah 31:1)

But he answered and said, "Assuredly, I say to you, I do not know you." (Matthew 25:12)

Our Model, David, Was a Man after God's Heart

But now your kingdom shall not continue. The Lord has sought for Himself a man after His own heart, and the Lord has commanded him [David] *to be commander* over His people, because you have not kept what the Lord commanded you. (1 Samuel 13:14)

And when He had removed him, He raised up for them David as king, to whom also He gave testimony and said, "I have found David the son of Jesse, *a man after My own heart, who will do all My will.*" (Acts 13:22)

For David says concerning Him: "I foresaw the Lord always before my face, for He is at my right hand, that I may not be shaken. . . . You have made known to me the ways of life; You will make me full of joy in Your presence." (Acts 2:25, 28)

David Wrote:

One *thing* I have desired of the Lord, that will I seek: that I may dwell in the house of the Lord all the days of my life, to behold the beauty of the Lord, and to inquire in

His temple. . . . *When You said,* "Seek My face," my heart said to You, "Your face, LORD, I will seek." (Psalm 27:4, 8)

I have set the LORD always before me; because He is at my right hand I shall not be moved. . . . You will show me the path of life; in Your presence *is* fullness of joy; at Your right hand are pleasures forevermore. (Psalm 16:8, 11)

God Will Accept Us as We Look to Know Him

But from there you will seek the LORD your God, and you will find *Him* if you seek Him with all your heart and with all your soul. (Deuteronomy 4:29)

But *it is* good for me to draw near to God; I have put my trust in the Lord GOD, that I may declare all Your works. (Psalm 73:28)

Seek the LORD and live. (Amos 5:6a)

And He has made from one blood every nation of men to dwell on all the face of the earth, and has determined their preappointed times and the boundaries of their dwellings, so that they should seek the Lord, in the hope that they might grope for Him and find Him, though He is not far from each one of us. (Acts 17:26–27)

Draw near to God and He will draw near to you. Cleanse *your* hands, *you* sinners; and purify *your* hearts, *you* double-minded. (James 4:8)

We Get to Know God by Encountering Him, Learning of Him, Experiencing Him, Knowing Him—Seeing Him

Take My yoke upon you and learn from Me, for I am gentle and lowly in heart, and you will find rest for your souls. (Matthew 11:29)

That I may know Him and the power of His resurrection, and the fellowship of His sufferings, being conformed to His death. (Philippians 3:10)

Beloved, now we are children of God; and it has not yet been revealed what we shall be, but we know that when He is revealed, we shall be like Him, for we shall see Him as He is. (1 John 3:2)

Knowing God, as He Knows Us, Is the Perfect Completion of Our Intimacy

For now we see in a mirror, dimly, but then *face to face.* Now I know in part, but then I shall know just as I also am known. (1 Corinthians 13:12)

Notes

Notes

10 Bible Stories Illustrating Immanuel Principles

One of the questions I have been asked about the Immanuel Approach is "Why, if this is real, don't I see Jesus or Paul doing it with believers?" We have no way of knowing if Jesus or Paul prayed for memories, but when Jesus freed Mary Magdalene from seven demons and set the Gadarene demoniac free, don't you picture them completely free—the pain removed from memories of their tortured pasts?

> And there are also many other things that Jesus did, which if they were written one by one, I suppose that even the world itself could not contain the books that would be written. Amen. (John 21:25)

Although we don't know everything Jesus did, we do know that *Immanuel* principles are incorporated into many Bible stories. Here are a few I've discovered.

I. Stephen's Stoning

Steven's stoning in the New Testament is a clear picture of the principles of the Immanuel Approach.

> But he, being full of the Holy Spirit, gazed into heaven and saw the glory of God, and Jesus standing at the right hand of God, and said, "Look! I see the heavens opened and the Son of Man standing at the right hand of God!"
>
> Then they cried out with a loud voice, stopped their ears, and ran at him with one accord; and they cast *him*

out of the city and stoned *him*. And the witnesses laid down their clothes at the feet of a young man named Saul. And they stoned Stephen as he was calling on *God* and saying, "Lord Jesus, receive my spirit." Then he knelt down and cried out with a loud voice, "Lord, do not charge them with this sin." And when he had said this, he fell asleep. (Acts 7:55–60)

Stephen sees Jesus. Jesus captures Stephen's full attention. With his eyes and mind on the Lord, Stephen moves into peace. Instead of a variety of emotions, Stephen displays the character of Jesus. He overcomes in the circumstances, just as Jesus overcame the world. When we see Jesus in an *Immanuel* session, we may be in painful difficult situations. Jesus does not fix them (the world), but he heals us so that we can overcome. Like Stephen, we come into peace and mirror Christlike character in giving heartfelt forgiveness and compassion to those who originally hurt us.

II. Jacob Wrestles with God

Jacob's wrestling with what is commonly thought to be an appearance of the preincarnate Christ illustrates another principle of *Immanuel*. Jacob, troubled by an expected clash with his brother, finds himself alone. A Man appears and they wrestle with each other. Jacob perseveres knowing that this Man can bless him. At the end, Jacob is defeated—to his great blessing. Now that his hip is disabled, he is reminded of his increased dependence on God with each step he takes.

Then Jacob was left alone; and a Man wrestled with him until the breaking of day. Now when He saw that He did not prevail against him, He touched the socket of his hip; and the socket of Jacob's hip was out of joint as He wrestled with him. And He said, "Let Me go, for the day breaks."

But he said, "I will not let You go unless You bless me!" So He said to him, "What is your name?" He said, "Jacob."

And He said, "Your name shall no longer be called Jacob, but Israel; for you have struggled with God and with men, and have prevailed."

Then Jacob asked, saying, "Tell *me* Your name, I pray." And He said, "Why *is* it *that* you ask about My name?" And He blessed him there.

So Jacob called the name of the place Peniel: "For I have seen God face to face, and my life is preserved." Just as he crossed over Penuel the sun rose on him, and he limped on his hip. (Genesis 32:24–31)

This often happens in *Immanuel* memory work. Our problems are overwhelming and seem impossible to fix, but we don't let go until Jesus helps. "**I need more help.**" He helps not by fixing the world, but by changing us. We quit thinking about the problem and become completely taken up by him. When this happens, we experience peace and joy. We stop striving and allow ourselves to become totally dependent on God.

III. Hannah Bares Her Soul to God

Hannah poured out her soul to God. So intense was her prayer that the High Priest Eli thought that she was drunk. She was in bitterness and anguish. She knew God well enough to trust him with all she was thinking, and no doubt it was not all pretty. While we don't know if she saw Jesus, she connected with God enough to believe the answer delivered by Eli, his representative. She went away in peace. She was not pregnant with the baby but with hope in God.

> And she [Hannah] *was* in bitterness of soul, and prayed to the LORD and wept in anguish. Then she made a vow and said, "O LORD of hosts, if You will indeed look on the affliction of Your maidservant and remember me, and not forget Your maidservant, but will give Your maidservant a male child, then I will give him to the LORD all the days of his life, and no razor shall come upon his head."
>
> And it happened, as she continued praying before the LORD, that Eli watched her mouth. Now Hannah spoke in her heart; only her lips moved, but her voice was not heard. Therefore Eli thought she was drunk. So Eli said to her, "How long will you be drunk? Put your wine away from you!"
>
> But Hannah answered and said, "No, my lord, I am a woman of sorrowful spirit. I have drunk neither wine nor intoxicating drink, but have poured out my soul before the LORD. Do not consider your maidservant a wicked woman, for out of the abundance of my complaint and grief I have spoken until now."

Then Eli answered and said, "Go in peace, and the God of Israel grant your petition which you have asked of Him."

And she said, "Let your maidservant find favor in your sight." So the woman went her way and ate, and her face was no longer *sad.* (1 Samuel 1:10–18)

It's amazing that an encounter with *Immanuel* can change us, even when it doesn't seem to change our circumstances. We are to be like Hannah; as we are honest with God, saying what's in our hearts to him, we find intimacy, truth, and freedom with *Immanuel.*

IV. David's Life with God

David's life wonderfully illustrates inner healing as a by-product of intimacy. His relationship with God in Psalms 16 and 27 mirrors what we experience in *Immanuel.*

A. David Brings His Pain to God

First, David brings his pain to God. His honest discourse with God models intimacy. He is not shy about telling God exactly how he feels.

Attend to me, and hear me; I mourn in my complaint, and make a noise. (Psalm 55:2, KJV)

B. David Asks God for Help

Second, David asks God for help to search for unknown wounds, lies, and sin.

> Search me, O God, and know my heart; try me, and know my anxieties; and see if there is any wicked way in me, and lead me in the way everlasting. (Psalm 139:23–24)

C. David Recognizes God's Will

Third, David recognizes what God wants. We see this in *Immanuel*. God wants truth to set us free. To get there, Jesus takes us to traumatic memories and reveals what really happened, including his unfailing presence and love.

> Behold, You desire truth in the inward parts, and in the hidden *part* You will make me to know wisdom. (Psalm 51:6)

In *Immanuel*, Jesus helps us to discover truth as he shines his light on both the dark places of our memories and our present misunderstandings and lies.

D. David Seeks Forgiveness

Fourth, in all humility, David cries out for God's forgiveness because he has sinned before God and against God. David recognizes that only God can resolve and restore their relationship. Only God can wash him clean from his sin.

Have mercy upon me, O God, according to Your loving-kindness; according to the multitude of Your tender mercies, blot out my transgressions. Wash me thoroughly from my iniquity, and cleanse me from my sin. For I acknowledge my transgressions, and my sin *is* always before me. Against You, You only, have I sinned, and done this evil in Your sight—that You may be found just when You speak, and blameless when You judge. . . . Create in me a clean heart, O God, and renew a steadfast spirit within me. (Psalm 51:1–4, 10)

In *Immanuel*, when we return to memories with Jesus, he sometimes opens our eyes to see our sin or to see events as they actually happened, even when we may remember them differently. It's part of our human nature (remember Adam?) to tend to blame everyone else. It takes grace, courage, and humility to let Jesus show us what really happened in our distorted memories. We get caught in our own deception, and Jesus is the only one who can bring truth, judge justly, and forgive. God creates a clean heart in us and restores righteousness.

E. David Longs for God

Fifth, David longs to see the Lord. He was a man after God's heart. He longs to be with God every day of his life. He longs to ask Jesus about things and to behold his beauty—to see him. He makes it his highest priority.

One *thing* I have desired of the LORD, that will I seek: that I may dwell in the house of the LORD all the days of my

life, to behold the beauty of the LORD, and to inquire in
His temple. (Psalm 27:4)

In *Immanuel*, we choose to be with Jesus. We set aside time
to ask him what he wants us to know. We see him as he really
is and as we discover truth about him, he becomes more and
more precious to us.

F. God Is David's Security and Solution

Sixth, David knows just how safe God is; he knows God is his
shelter. He knows his God and knows that God would be able
to save him from trouble.

For in the time of trouble He shall hide me in His pavilion; in the secret place of His tabernacle He shall hide me;
He shall set me high upon a rock. (Psalm 27:5)

When we are overwhelmed, both in our current lives and in
unresolved places from our past, Jesus takes us to the source of
our trouble and opens our eyes to see that he has always been
with us and is with us now. He always overcomes the world by
bringing us into truth and drawing us to himself. He always is
the unexpected solution.

G. David's Devotion to God

Seventh, David sets God before him every day; he recognizes
that God is always with him, at his right hand. This knowledge

gives David strength for the day. When David is in God's presence, he is full of joy.

> I have set the LORD always before me; because He is at my right hand I shall not be moved. . . .You will show me the path of life; in Your presence *is* fullness of joy; at Your right hand *are* pleasures forevermore. (Psalm 16:8, 11)

In *Immanuel*, we learn that we too can set Jesus before us; we can open to the Spirit's revelation and practice his presence. Because of the secure attachment we develop from daily life experiences in his presence, we have a secure foundation for all our relationships. We are not moved because he is not moved.

V. God's Presence with Shadrach, Meshach, and Abed-Nego

When Shadrach, Meshach, and Abed–Nego were thrown into the firey furnace, Jesus appeared and they knew that he was with them. Jesus did not change their situation but overcame it. They were not burned, but freed.

> Therefore, because the king's command was urgent, and the furnace exceedingly hot, the flame of the fire killed those men who took up Shadrach, Meshach, and Abed–Nego. And these three men, Shadrach, Meshach, and Abed–Nego, fell down bound into the midst of the burning fiery furnace.
>
> Then King Nebuchadnezzar was astonished; and he rose in haste and spoke, saying to his counselors, "Did we not cast three men bound into the midst of the fire?"

V. God's Presence with Shadrach, Meshach, and Abed-Nego (cont.)

They answered and said to the king, "True, O king."

"Look!" he answered, "I see four men loose, walking in the midst of the fire; and they are not hurt, and the form of the fourth is like the Son of God."

Then Nebuchadnezzar went near the mouth of the burning fiery furnace *and* spoke, saying, "Shadrach, Meshach, and Abed–Nego, servants of the Most High God, come out, and come *here.*" Then Shadrach, Meshach, and Abed–Nego came from the midst of the fire.

And the satraps, administrators, governors, and the king's counselors gathered together, and they saw these men on whose bodies the fire had no power; the hair of their head was not singed nor were their garments affected, and the smell of fire was not on them.

Nebuchadnezzar spoke, saying, "Blessed be the God of Shadrach, Meshach, and Abed–Nego, who sent His Angel and delivered His servants who trusted in Him. (Daniel 3:22–28a)

This is reminiscent of Jesus' presence in overwhelming memories. He is always with us. Because of his presence, we are set free, even though he doesn't change what happened to us.

VI. The Samaritan Woman Encounters Jesus

The woman at the well encountered Jesus. In that encounter, Immanuel answered her questions by revealing who he is.

The woman said to Him, "Sir, I perceive that You are a prophet. Our fathers worshiped on this mountain, and you *Jews* say that in Jerusalem is the place where one ought to worship."

Jesus said to her, "Woman, believe Me, the hour is coming when you will neither on this mountain, nor in Jerusalem, worship the Father. You worship what you do not know; we know what we worship, for salvation is of the Jews. But the hour is coming, and now is, when the true worshipers will worship the Father in spirit and truth; for the Father is seeking such to worship Him. God *is* Spirit, and those who worship Him must worship in spirit and truth."

The woman said to Him, "I know that Messiah is coming" (who is called Christ). "When He comes, He will tell us all things."

Jesus said to her, "I who speak to you am He." (John 4:19–26)

We get answers in our conversations with Jesus during *Immanuel* sessions. Usually, the answers are much bigger than our original concerns. It's like the woman at the well; she asks about the correct place of worship, and Jesus reveals that he is the Messiah, the Worshipped One. As always, he is the answer and he is all that matters.

VII. Jesus Walks on the Water

When the disciples saw Jesus walking on the water, they weren't sure who he was. Peter was willing to risk getting out of the boat and walk on the water if—it was indeed Jesus who was there.

VII. Jesus Walks on the Water (cont.)

> Now in the fourth watch of the night Jesus went to them, walking on the sea. And when the disciples saw Him walking on the sea, they were troubled, saying, "It is a ghost!" And they cried out for fear.
>
> But immediately Jesus spoke to them, saying, "Be of good cheer! It is I; do not be afraid."
>
> And Peter answered Him and said, *"Lord, if it is You,* command me to come to You on the water."
>
> So He said, "Come." And when Peter had come down out of the boat, he walked on the water to go to Jesus. (Matthew 14:25–29)

Many people are afraid to see Jesus for fear of doing something wrong. Once, however, they know it's really Jesus calling them into intimacy, they are willing to "walk on the water." They are willing to see and experience him. They are willing to go to dark places of memory with him too.

VIII. Abraham Bargains with God

Abraham questioned God and bargained with him over how many righteous people living in Sodom would save the city from destruction.

> And the LORD said, "Shall I hide from Abraham what I am doing?
>
> Then the men turned away from there and went toward Sodom, but Abraham still stood before the LORD. And

Abraham came near and said, "Would You also destroy the righteous with the wicked? Suppose there were fifty righteous within the city; would You also destroy the place and not spare *it* for the fifty righteous that were in it? Far be it from You to do such a thing as this, to slay the righteous with the wicked, so that the righteous should be as the wicked; far be it from You! Shall not the Judge of all the earth do right?"

So the LORD said, "If I find in Sodom fifty righteous within the city, then I will spare all the place for their sakes."

Then Abraham answered and said, "Indeed now, I who *am* but dust and ashes have taken it upon myself to speak to the Lord." . . .

Then he said, "Let not the Lord be angry, and I will speak but once more: Suppose ten should be found there?"

And He said, "I will not destroy it for the sake of ten." So the LORD went His way as soon as He had finished speaking with Abraham; and Abraham returned to his place. (Genesis 18:17, 22–27, 32–33)

In *Immanuel*, we "reason together" with Jesus about conditions that make us feel safe enough to take risks with him. (Isaiah 1:18)

IX. A Blind Man Healed by Jesus

The blind man was questioned by the religious authorities because Jesus healed him. They couldn't believe he was healed

IX. A Blind Man Healed by Jesus (cont.)

because it didn't fit into their religious beliefs. But the evidence proves the truth.

> Now as Jesus passed by, He saw a man who was blind from birth. . . .
>
> And He said to him, "Go, wash in the pool of Siloam" (which is translated, Sent). So he went and washed, and came back seeing. . . .
>
> He answered and said, "Whether He is a sinner *or not* I do not know. One thing I know: that though I was blind, now I see." . . .
>
> Then they said to him again, "What did He do to you? How did He open your eyes?" . . .
>
> "Since the world began it has been unheard of that anyone opened the eyes of one who was born blind. If this Man were not from God, He could do nothing." (John 9:1, 7, 25–26, 32–33)

When we are changed, healed, and freed through *Immanuel*, people sometimes question it. They may not believe that we have intimacy with Immanuel or that he has healed us—even though the change is obvious to everyone who knows us. Sometimes telling others that we've been with Jesus doesn't satisfy questioners who can't believe that God is near and involved in our well-being. Sometimes I just have to leave it with, "I was blind, but now I see."

X. The Death of Lazarus—Martha's Response

Martha began with blame. Four days after her brother Lazarus's death she met Jesus on the way to their home in Bethany. She was beside herself with grief and accused Jesus of coming too late to save Lazarus. He talks with her and she comes to know Jesus for who he really is.

> Now Martha, as soon as she heard that Jesus was coming, went and met Him, but Mary was sitting in the house. Then Martha said to Jesus, "Lord, if You had been here, my brother would not have died. But even now I know that whatever You ask of God, God will give You."
>
> Jesus said to her, "Your brother will rise again."
>
> Martha said to Him, "I know that he will rise again in the resurrection at the last day."
>
> Jesus said to her, "I am the resurrection and the life. He who believes in Me, though he may die, he shall live. And whoever lives and believes in Me shall never die. Do you believe this?"
>
> She said to Him, "Yes, Lord, I believe that You are the Christ, the Son of God, who is to come into the world." (John 11:20–27)

When Jesus takes us to hidden memories where we are overwhelmed, we often blame God for what happened. This blame comes as a surprise to most of us, but in the heat of the emotions, it surfaces. Jesus isn't discouraged or put off by our wounds and lies. He is able to work with them so that in the end we can see truth. He is our salvation and comforter in every situation.

XI. The Death of Lazarus—Mary's Response

Mary and Jesus were attuned to one another. Mary, from the same story, came to Jesus weeping after the death of her brother, Lazarus. She, too, knew that Jesus could have prevented his death, but Jesus handled her response differently. He wept. He attuned to her in her distress. Remember, they were already close as teacher and disciple. The Jews (professional mourners at the funeral) thought that Jesus was weeping because of his own pain at losing his friend, but he instead he was weeping with Mary. Jesus knew Lazarus was going to be resurrected. He wasn't experiencing a loss. All of his attention was on Mary, and he was experiencing her pain with her.

> Then, when Mary came where Jesus was, and saw Him, she fell down at His feet, saying to Him, "Lord, if You had been here, my brother would not have died."
>
> Therefore, when Jesus saw her weeping, and the Jews who came with her weeping, He groaned in the spirit and was troubled. And He said, "Where have you laid him?"
>
> They said to Him, "Lord, come and see."
>
> Jesus wept. Then the Jews said, "See how He loved him!" And some of them said, "Could not this Man, who opened the eyes of the blind, also have kept this man from dying?" (John 11:32–37)

Immanuel is so much about attunement. When Jesus attunes to us, nothing else seems to matter. He knows our frames; he knows our struggles; he knows our thoughts. And he loves us. He is able to heal us in the midst of the worst of circumstances simply by being truly with us.

XII. Jesus Washes the Disciples' Feet

When Jesus finished the last Passover meal with the disciples, he wraps a towel around his waist and washes their feet. Peter objects and says that he needs to be washed all over. Jesus reminds him that he is already clean, and only needs his feet washed. Jesus tells his disciples to wash one another's feet just as he had washed theirs. He tells them that he is their model of how to live. He tells them that there is a blessing for disciples with humility enough to serve others as he served them.

[Jesus] rose from supper and laid aside His garments, took a towel and girded Himself. After that, He poured water into a basin and began to wash the disciples' feet, and to wipe *them* with the towel with which He was girded. Then He came to Simon Peter. And *Peter* said to Him, "Lord, are You washing my feet?"

Jesus answered and said to him, "What I am doing you do not understand now, but you will know after this."

Peter said to Him, "You shall never wash my feet!"

Jesus answered him, "If I do not wash you, you have no part with Me."

Simon Peter said to Him, "Lord, not my feet only, but also *my* hands and *my* head!"

Jesus said to him, "He who is bathed needs only to wash *his* feet, but is completely clean; and you are clean, but not all of you." For He knew who would betray Him; therefore He said, "You are not all clean."

So when He had washed their feet, taken His garments, and sat down again, He said to them, "Do you know what I have done to you? You call me Teacher and Lord, and you say well, for *so* I am. If I then, *your* Lord and Teacher, have washed your feet, you also ought to wash one another's feet. For I have given you an example, that you should do as I have done to you. Most assuredly, I say to you, a servant is not greater than his master; nor is he who is sent greater than he who sent him. If you know these things, blessed are you if you do them." (John 13:4–17)

In *Immanuel*, Jesus comes not to save us again, but to wipe off the dust (wounds, lies, and sin) that we pick up as we walk through this life. He gently washes us clean of the day-to-day disruptions to his gracious plans for us and to our intimacy with him. Then he encourages us to do this for one another. Once we learn the simple principles of *Immanuel*, we can bring each other to Jesus to get washed and receive His forgiveness, deliverance, healing, and freedom. These are great blessings for both the coach and the receiver.

XIII. Conclusion

Holy Spirit frequently uses Bible stories to explain my experience during *Immanuel* sessions. Jesus says or does something and I will realize that it's not new—"this is that!" (see Acts 2:16, KJV)—it's in a familiar Bible story. *Immanuel* principles can be found throughout the Bible. I invite you to share the stories the Holy Spirit shows you with me and others you know.

Notes

I've heard lots of stories about about Jesus appearing to people who have never even heard heard his name. Some were about people in China, India, even some appearances to Native Americans. Here are a few stories about Jesus appearing to Muslims in our times.

I. The "JESUS" Film Project

Dear Friend in Christ,

Declare with the psalmist of old: "Let all the earth fear the Lord; let all the inhabitants of the world stand in awe of Him" (Psalm 33:8, New American Standard Bible).

As you are about to read, He is marvelously present and active . . . calling out His body from among the most difficult of places.

You may remember how I wrote to you a couple of months ago about a recent, terrible flood in a highly restricted nation. "JESUS" film teams had gone out with boats to rescue as many people as possible. They risked everything to reach them. And once safe, they showed the people "JESUS."

In one of those places the waters were steadily rising. One by one, everyone left their homes, with only hours before they were hopelessly cut off. Everyone left, but one lone man.

He was a maker of suicide vests and bombs. His home was in the center of radical activity, a "workshop of death," filled with explosives of all kinds . . . wiring, vests and detonators. He too wanted to leave. But then word came down from a top radical leader that he was to stay and protect the explosives at all cost, even with his life. He obeyed.

So there he remained in the silence, alone, behind his locked door, fearing he was about to drown. Suddenly, there was an authoritative knock, a banging at the door. Feeling compelled to respond, he unlatched and opened the door. Immediately, the waters rushed in, swamping and ruining all his tools of death.

But before him was an amazing sight—a man dressed in brilliant white, who said, "Stop protecting these things that destroy. Follow me."

Thinking the man in white was a religious leader of a very high order, he obeyed and began walking with him, hand in hand.

When he arrived on dry land where the people had gathered, they were amazed. They asked, how did you cross the flood, how did you survive? He explained how the man in brilliant white had led him out, and they crossed the flood by walking on the water. He couldn't even believe what had just happened. It was like a dream.

Knowing that God may have indeed just saved his life, film workers arranged to show him the film "JESUS." When he saw Jesus portrayed in the film, the bomb maker shouted out, *"That's the Man!!"*

Now, teams working in this difficult area report that upwards of fifty percent of all new believers come to faith after experiencing a vision, dream or appearance of Jesus. When the workers hear them mention the "man in white" they show the film, and it is not uncommon that they respond the same way: *"That's the Man!"*

You may rightly ask, "Why does Jesus appear in this way?" "Why visions?" Perhaps it's because the chains of spiritual darkness and oppression are so strong. Only Jesus can overpower demonic prisons of deception. Further, some have asked if we believe that the historic Jesus actually looked like the man chosen to play Jesus. No, but we do believe that the Holy Spirit causes this association in appearance to verify the Truth to people who live in these oppressive areas.

In fact, the Risen Lord has appeared to so many. The teams have often shown the film in response. It is believed in one area (that is also a center of terrorism) there are now 20,000 followers of Jesus as a result of people experiencing the "JESUS" film! In addition, sixty new believers are now engaged in theological studies to lead newly formed churches or small groups. Many of them were once part of a well-known terrorist organization. When asked why they are risking so much, even death, they reply, "Because we have found the Truth."*

* "Showing God's Love to the World", Newsletter August 3, 2011 (revised 11/8/11), The "JESUS" Film Project, a ministry of Campus Crusade for Christ, 100 Lake Hart Road, Orlando, Florida 32832, www.jesusfilm.org. Reprinted with permission.

II. Chris Mitchell, CBN News Middle East Bureau Chief

"There is an end-time phenomenon that is happening through dreams and visions," said Christine Darg, author of *The Jesus Visions: Signs and Wonders in the Muslim World.* "He is going into the Muslim world and revealing, particularly, the last twenty-four hours of His life—how He died on the cross, which Islam does not teach—how He was raised from the dead, which Islam also does not teach—how He is the Son of God, risen in power."

"We receive lots of letters about people who have had dreams about the Lord, visions, even miracles," [Nazir] Shaheen [host of a Christian program] said. "When they watch the program, they say yes, we had a dream or a vision, and they accept Jesus as Lord."†

† Chris Mitchell, "Visions of Jesus Stir Muslim Hearts," *CBN World News,* Monday, August 13, 2007, http://www.cbn.com /cbnnews/world/2008/Visions-of-Jesus-Stir-Muslim-Hearts/. Used with permission.

III. Sid Roth Interview with Joel Richardson

Sid: Tell me one testimony of a Muslim that came to the Lord, just briefly.

Joel: Well, this story is—I love it—it is actually a whole village. I heard this one recently where there were some missionaries coming to a remote village, and they were going to show the *Jesus* film. As they set up their stands and they were showing [the film to] the village, when they got to the scene of the crucifixion, the people were just beating their chests and screaming and just incredibly emotional. And when they had a translator they found out what happened is that in the weeks before the missionaries came there was a man who showed up in the village, and he had been preaching the gospel to them. And when they saw the movie it was the man from the movie that had been in their village. Jesus himself had appeared to these villagers in the form of the actor from the movie. He revealed Himself that way. He was preaching the gospel to them. When the missionaries came, they recognized that that was the man that had been in the village. The people understood the gospel and the whole village became believers.[§]

§ Sid Roth, "Sid Roth Welcomes Joel Richardson," *Sid-Roth.com*, August 19, 2011, http://www.sid-roth.com/2011/08/19/sid-roth -welcomes-joel-richardson-5/.

Perhaps these stories are sensational enough to give a good answer to the nagging question, "But what about the people who never hear? Surely God would give them a chance to accept his gracious offer. After all Jesus died for them and belief in him and his work is all they need to be with God forever." For that, he knows the best strategy (Acts 17:26–27).

Another concern are the Westerners who just don't need God—or so they think. They are just as lost as Muslims, Hindus, and others who've never heard of him and are without God. For instance, I grew up in a mainline American church and had no idea of the content of the gospel. Jesus was comfortably on the sidelines of my life.

III. This Is My Story

At twenty-seven years old, I had everything I had ever hoped for. My husband, baby twin daughters, and I had just moved to a new town upon Mike's appointment as a law clerk to a federal district judge. I knew no one and had no car, but that was okay because with twins I only did babies! Shortly after moving, the girls and I met the woman across the street while out walking. She invited us to dinner that night.

After a really good dinner, the discussion over dishes was about that day's *Phil Donahue Show.* Phil's guest was the Preacher of Bourbon Street. "Can you believe the number of people who don't believe in the Devil?" she asked. Whoa. I didn't believe— we didn't believe. Maybe some evil force, but not the cartoon character with the red suit, pitchfork, and smoke.

As I spoke, her husband's hand went slowly across the counter to a black book. (Later, I learned that he was a Pentecostal Holiness pastor.) He tucked it under his arm invited us to the family room. He started talking about the devil and opened his Bible to the last book, Revelation. It began to storm: thunder, lightning, pouring down rain. That is, "all ___ broke loose!" I got the good old ghost story chills. And yes, I was interested, but more polite than glued to his sharing. When it stopped storming, we said good night and took the babies home for bed. As we were leaving, he asked if I had a Bible. I looked at Mike. Doesn't everybody—but us? He sent his home with us until I could locate ours. Perhaps we'd like to read some of it?

Now with two babies, you quickly learn to sleep when they do. But after putting them down, I couldn't sleep. I kept thinking about that black book on the table in the den. So I got up, turned to Revelation and started to read. It made no sense to me. I persevered until Revelation 3:20, "Behold, I stand at the door and knock." The words went electric as a man standing behind my right shoulder read them to me. Somehow, I knew this man was Jesus. I knew what he looked like and how he sounded. He moved from behind my back and sat down in the chair across from mine. His demeanor was friendly and casual. I don't know what we first talked about, but at the end of the conversation, Jesus said, "If you give me control of your life, I will rule your life." I knew immediately that this had something to do with my heart. To my surprise, I responded, "OK." Then I thought again. I said, "But I don't even know that you are real." And he said, "If I'm not real, this conversation won't make any difference, but if I am real, it will make all the difference."

He disappeared and I, being a someone who has to finish, tried to finish the chapter. I was suddenly so tired that I closed the book and went to bed.

I didn't know then, but soon realized that our conversation did indeed make all the difference. *He is real!*

◈ Notes

Preface

1. See appendix 4, "Experiencing God."

2. See appendix 9, "God Accepts and Loves Intimacy with Us."

3. "Heal the sick, cleanse the lepers, raise the dead, cast out demons. Freely you have received, freely give" (Matthew 10:8).

Chapter One: Beginning Questions

1. "Repent therefore and be converted, that your sins may be blotted out, so that times of refreshing may come from the presence of the Lord, and that He may send Jesus Christ, who was preached to you before" (Acts 3:19–20).

2. "As Christ also loved the church and gave Himself for her, that He might sanctify and cleanse her with the washing of water by the word, that He might present her to Himself a glorious church, not having spot or wrinkle or any such thing, but that she should be holy and without blemish" (Ephesians 5:25b–27).

3. "Beloved, now we are children of God; and it has not yet been revealed what we shall be, but we know that when He is revealed, we shall be like Him, for we shall see Him as He is." (1 John 3:2)

4. "For whom He foreknew, He also predestined *to be* conformed to the image of His Son, that He might be the firstborn among many brethren" (Romans 8:29).

5. In the real world, stuff from the coach and the receiver leaks in, but our goal is for Jesus to be the leader and provide all of the direction with respect to content and solution.

6. Karl Lehman, *Outsmarting Yourself: Catching Your Past Invading the Present and What to Do about It* (Libertyville, IL: This Joy! Books, 2011), 72.

7. "Let us be glad and rejoice and give Him glory, for the marriage of the Lamb has come, and His wife has made herself ready" (Revelation 19:7).

8. "For I am jealous for you with godly jealousy. For I have betrothed you to one husband, that I may present *you as* a chaste virgin to Christ" (2 Corinthians 11:2).

9. The coach often feels like things move more slowly and less efficiently when she keeps quiet and defers leadship to Jesus, but when we watch carefully over time, we often discover that Jesus knows what he's doing. When all the pieces come together at the end, we see that Jesus actually gets to the finish line more quickly and with a much more elegant result.

10. "But now indeed *there are* many members, yet one body. And the eye cannot say to the hand, 'I have no need of you;' nor again the head to the feet, 'I have no need of you'" (1 Corinthians 12:20–21).

11. "Confess *your* trespasses to one another, and pray for one another, that you may be healed. The effective, fervent prayer of a righteous man avails much" (James 5:16).

Chapter Two: Getting Started

1. "And Enoch walked with God; and he *was* not, for God took him" (Genesis 5:24).

2. "If you diligently heed the voice of the LORD your God and do what is right in His sight, give ear to His commandments and keep all His statutes, I will put none of the diseases on you which I have brought on the Egyptians. For I *am* the LORD who heals you" (Exodus 15:26).

3. There's a distinction between leading the *process* (which is indeed what the coach is supposed to do), and leading with respect to agenda, content, memories, clever ideas for facilitating healing, and so forth, which is what the Lord does. The coach is there for support, attunement, provision, and focus on Jesus.

Chapter Three: Greeting

1. Dr. Karl Lehman and most experienced therapists and *Immanuel* facilitators do not worry about where they might end up in a session or whether they will be able to handle the situation if the person temporarily gets stuck in a difficult place. He observes,

> An important point here: establishing the connection with Jesus at the beginning of the session is an important safety net for beginners and for group settings. This is one of the safety nets that makes it possible to do *Immanuel* group exercises, and why I feel safe encouraging lay people to try *Immanuel*, even though they have no prior experience or training with respect to emotional healing. And this is one of the safety nets that will protect *Immanuel* from the unfortunate "disasters" that sometimes occur when beginners get in over their heads with other approaches to emotional healing. . . . Making sure the person starts the session with first connecting to Jesus is an important safety net for beginners and groups—if the recipient gets stuck later in the session for one reason or another, and the beginner coach is not able to troubleshoot effectively enough to get unstuck, they can always go back to the place of positive connection with Jesus established at the beginning of the session. This is why, when we do group exercises, we instruct the small group teams to only do trauma work with participants who have been able to establish a positive connection with Jesus at the beginning of the exercise (so that they have this safety net to come back to)."

See Karl Lehman, "Brain Science, Psychological Trauma, and the God Who Is With Us: Part V, The Immanuel Approach Revisited" for discussion of additional safety nets for *Immanuel* in group settings.

Chapter Four: Opening Prayer

1. "Likewise you younger people, submit yourselves to *your* elders. Yes, all of *you* be submissive to one another, and be clothed with humility, for *'God resists the proud, but gives grace to the humble'*" (1 Peter 5:5).

2. "And Jesus came and spoke to them, saying, 'All authority has been given to Me in heaven and on earth'" (Matthew 28:18).

3. "For God is not *the author* of confusion but of peace" (1 Corinthians 14:33a).

4. "For it seemed good to the Holy Spirit, and to us" (Acts 15:28a).

5. "For I say, through the grace given to me, to everyone who is among you, not to think *of himself* more highly than he ought to think, but to think soberly, as God has dealt to each one a measure of faith" (Romans 12:3).

Chapter Five: Focusing on Jesus

1. "For your Father knows the things you have need of before you ask Him" (Matthew 6:8b).

2. "You will keep *him* in perfect peace, *whose* mind *is* stayed *on You*, because he trusts in You" (Isaiah 26:3).

3. "Now we are sure that You know all things, and have no need that anyone should question You. By this we believe that You came forth from God" (John 16:30).

4. "Enter into His gates with thanksgiving, *and* into His courts with praise. Be thankful to Him, *and* bless His name" (Psalm 100:4).

5. "Jesus Christ *is* the same yesterday, today, and forever" (Hebrews 13:8).

"For I *am* the LORD, I do not change; therefore you are not consumed, O sons of Jacob" (Malachi 3:6).

6. "Therefore the Lord Himself will give you a sign: Behold, the virgin shall conceive and bear a Son, and shall call His name Immanuel" (Isaiah 7:14).

"Behold, the virgin shall be with child, and bear a Son, and they shall call His name Immanuel," which is translated, "God with us" (Matthew 1:23).

7. "Where can I go from Your Spirit? Or where can I flee from Your presence?" (Psalm 139:7).

8. "But you are not in the flesh but in the Spirit, if indeed the Spirit of God dwells in you. Now if anyone does not have the Spirit of Christ, he is not His" (Romans 8:9).

9. See appendix 7, "Why See?"

10. "But he who is joined to the Lord is one spirit *with Him*" (1 Corinthians 6:17).

"For by one Spirit we were all baptized into one body—whether Jews or Greeks, whether slaves or free—and have all been made to drink into one Spirit" (1 Corinthians 12:13).

11. "For through Him we both have access by one Spirit to the Father" (Ephesians 2:18).

12. "And not holding fast to the Head, from whom all the body, nourished and knit together by joints and ligaments, grows with the increase *that is* from God" (Colossians 2:19).

13. See appendix 3, "God with Us."

14. See appendix 8, "Objections to Seeing God."

15. "For now we see in a mirror, dimly, but then face to face. Now I know in part, but then I shall know just as I also am known" (1 Corinthians 13:12).

16. "The eyes of your understanding being enlightened; that you may know what is the hope of His calling, what are the riches of the glory of His inheritance in the saints" (Ephesians 1:18).

17. "But when the Helper comes, whom I shall send to you from the Father, the Spirit of truth who proceeds from the Father, He will testify of Me." (John 15:26)

18. "The Spirit of the LORD shall rest upon Him, the Spirit of wisdom and understanding, the Spirit of counsel and might, the Spirit of knowledge and of the fear of the LORD" (Isaiah 11:2).

19. See appendix 6, "God Can Appear in Different Forms."

20. "But solid food belongs to those who are of full age, *that is*, those who by reason of use have their senses exercised to discern both good and evil" (Hebrews 5:14).

"I write to you, little children, because your sins are forgiven you for His name's sake. I write to you, fathers, because you have known Him *who is* from the beginning. I write to you, young men, because you have overcome the wicked one. I write to you, little children, because you have known the Father. I have written to you, fathers, because you have known Him *who is* from the beginning. I have written to you, young men, because you are strong, and the word of God abides in you, and you have overcome the wicked one" (1 John 2:12–14).

21. "Looking unto Jesus, the author and finisher of *our* faith" (Hebrews 12:2a).

22. See appendix 5, "People in Scripture Who Saw God."

23. "Jesus . . . endured the cross, despising the shame, and has sat down at the right hand of the throne of God" (Hebrews 12:2b).

"Greater love has no one than this, than to lay down one's life for his friends" (John 15:13).

Chapter Six: Memory Work

1. "Behold, You desire truth in the inward parts, and in the hidden *part* You will make me to know wisdom" (Psalm 51:6).

2. "And you shall know the truth, and the truth shall make you free" (John 8:32).

3. "When my father and my mother forsake me, then the LORD will take care of me" (Psalm 27:10).

4. "For in You the fatherless finds mercy" (Hosea 14:3c).

5. "My times *are* in Your hand; deliver me from the hand of my enemies, and from those who persecute me" (Psalm 31:15).

6. "For My yoke *is* easy and My burden is light" (Matthew 11:30).

7. "For I know the thoughts that I think toward you, says the LORD, thoughts of peace and not of evil, to give you a future and a hope" (Jeremiah 29:11).

8. "Yea, though I walk through the valley of the shadow of death, I will fear no evil; for You *are* with me; Your rod and Your staff, they comfort me" (Psalm 23:4).

9. "When you pass through the waters, I *will be* with you; and through the rivers, they shall not overflow you. When you walk through the fire, you shall not be burned, nor shall the flame scorch you" (Isaiah 43:2).

10. "If you then, being evil, know how to give good gifts to your children, how much more will your Father who is in heaven give good things to those who ask Him!" (Matthew 7:11).

11. According to Dr. Karl, "With people, who consistently mess up, part of building secure attachment is having the consistent experience of adequate repair when the caregiver messes up. The child learns that the caregiver may temporarily fail with respect to one of the key needs, but that the caregiver will always then repair the problem."

12. "For He Himself has said, *'I will never leave you nor forsake you'*" (Hebrews 13:5b).

"Be strong and of good courage, do not fear nor be afraid of them; for the LORD your God, He *is* the One who goes with you. He will not leave you nor forsake you. . . . And the LORD, He *is* the One who goes before you. He will be with you, He will not leave you nor forsake you; do not fear nor be dismayed" (Deuteronomy 31:6, 8).

"No man shall *be able* to stand before you all the days of your life; as I was with Moses, *so* I will be with you. I will not leave you nor forsake you" (Joshua 1:5).

"'And lo, I am with you always, *even* to the end of the age.' Amen" (Matthew 28:20b).

13. "The steps of a *good* man are ordered by the LORD, and He delights in his way" (Psalm 37:23).

"You shall no longer be termed Forsaken, nor shall your land any more be termed Desolate; but you shall be called Hephzibah, and your land Beulah; for the LORD delights in you, and your land shall be married. For *as* a young man marries a virgin, *so* shall your sons marry you; and *as* the bridegroom rejoices over the bride, *so* shall your God rejoice over you" (Isaiah 62:4–5).

"The Lord your God in your midst, the Mighty One, will save; He will rejoice over you with gladness, He will quiet you with His love, He will rejoice over *you* with singing" (Zephaniah 3:17).

14. "Behold, God *is* my helper; the Lord *is* with those who uphold my life" (Psalm 54:4).

"The God of my strength, in whom I will trust; my shield and the horn of my salvation, my stronghold and my refuge; my Savior, You save me from violence" (2 Samuel 22:3).

"Paul, an apostle of Jesus Christ, by the commandment of God our Savior and the Lord Jesus Christ, our hope" (1 Timothy 1:1).

15. One exception we see to "a person's mind is never blank" is when internal parts are afraid of where the process might go and create a "total blank" as a way to block the process. As far as we can tell, people really do experience a blank—no extraneous thoughts, just a total blank, dark, wall. I teach about this because I see it occasionally, and want to avoid damaging people's credibility if they say it never happens (and then experience it). The response I teach for lay ministers is "coach the person to go back to the place where she can perceive Jesus, and then help her engage directly with Jesus regarding the blank." (Dr. Karl Lehman)

16. "For everyone who asks receives, and he who seeks finds, and to him who knocks it will be opened" (Matthew 7:8).

"And whatever things you ask in prayer, believing, you will receive" (Matthew 21:22).

17. See appendix 3, "God with Us."

18. "He who has My commandments and keeps them, it is he who loves Me. And he who loves Me will be loved by My Father, and I will love him and manifest Myself to him" (John 14:21).

Also see appendix 3, "God with Us."

19. "He restores my soul; He leads me in the paths of righteousness for His name's sake. Yea, though I walk through the valley of the shadow of death, I will fear no evil; for You *are* with me; Your rod and Your staff, they comfort me" (Psalm 23:3–4).

20. "Behold, I give you the authority to trample on serpents and scorpions, and over all the power of the enemy, and nothing shall by any means hurt you" (Luke 10:19).

21. "Therefore let us, as many as are mature, have this mind; and if in anything you think otherwise, God will reveal even this to you" (Philippians 3:15).

22. *God's original intent:* "Now therefore, if you will indeed obey My voice and keep My covenant, then you shall be a special treasure to Me above all people; for all the earth *is* Mine. And you shall be to Me a kingdom of priests and a holy nation" (Exodus 19:5–6a).

Man's refusal: "Then they said to Moses, 'You speak with us, and we will hear; but let not God speak with us, lest we die'" (Exodus 20:19).

God's restoration: "But you *are* a chosen generation, a royal priesthood, a holy nation, His own special people, that you may proclaim the praises of Him who called you out of darkness into His marvelous light" (1 Peter 2:9).

23. "Therefore comfort each other and edify one another, just as you also are doing" (1 Thessalonians 5:11).

24. "Come to Me, all *you* who labor and are heavy laden, and I will give you rest" (Matthew 11:28).

Chapter Seven: Healing

1. See appendix 10, "Bible Stories Illustrating Immanuel Principles."

2. See appendix 10, "Bible Stories Illustrating Immanuel Principles."

3. "But we all, with unveiled face, beholding as in a mirror the glory of the Lord, are being transformed into the same image from glory to glory, just as by the Spirit of the Lord" (2 Corinthians 3:18).

4. "These things I have spoken to you, that in Me you may have peace. In the world you will have tribulation; but be of good cheer, I have overcome the world." (John 16:33)

5. "He who sins is of the devil, for the devil has sinned from the beginning. For this purpose the Son of God was manifested, that He might destroy the works of the devil." (1 John 3:8)

6. "Jesus said to him, 'I am the way, the truth, and the life'" (John 14:6a).

7. "You will keep *him* in perfect peace, *whose* mind *is* stayed *on You*, because he trusts in You" (Isaiah 26:3).

8. "For the kingdom of God is not eating and drinking, but righteousness and peace and joy in the Holy Spirit" (Romans 14:17).

9. "And he believed in the LORD, and He accounted it to him for righteousness" (Genesis 15:6).

"For God so loved the world that He gave His only begotten Son, that whoever believes in Him should not perish but have everlasting life" (John 3:16).

"Therefore, having been justified by faith, we have peace with God through our Lord Jesus Christ" (Romans 5:1).

10. "And by Him to reconcile all things to Himself, by Him, whether things on earth or things in heaven, having made peace through the blood of His cross. And you, who once were alienated and enemies in your mind by wicked works, yet now He has reconciled in the body of His flesh through death, to present you holy, and blameless, and above reproach in His sight" (Colossians 1:20–22).

11. "If we say that we have fellowship with Him, and walk in darkness, we lie and do not practice the truth. But if we walk in the light as He is in the light, we have fellowship with one another, and the blood of Jesus Christ His Son cleanses us from all sin. If we say that we have no sin, we deceive ourselves, and the truth is not in us. If we confess our sins, He is faithful and just to forgive us *our* sins and to cleanse us from all unrighteousness" (1 John 1:6–9).

12. "Search me, O God, and know my heart; try me, and know my anxieties; and see if *there is any* wicked way in me, and lead me in the way everlasting" (Psalm 139:23–24).

"For with You *is* the fountain of life; in Your light we see light" (Psalm 36:9).

13. See appendix 11, "God Now Appearing to the Unbeliever."

14. "So I will restore to you the years that the swarming locust has eaten, the crawling locust, the consuming locust, and the chewing locust, My great army which I sent among you" (Joel 2:25).

15. "Beloved, I pray that you may prosper in all things and be in health, just as your soul prospers" (3 John 1:2).

16. "And having been set free from sin, you became slaves of righteousness" (Romans 6:18).

17. "There is no fear in love; but perfect love casts out fear, because fear involves torment. But he who fears has not been made perfect in love" (1 John 4:18).

18. "He restores my soul; He leads me in the paths of righteousness for His name's sake" (Psalm 23:3).

"Take My yoke upon you and learn from Me, for I am gentle and lowly in heart, and you will find rest for your souls" (Matthew 11:29).

19. "Both riches and honor *come* from You, and You reign over all. In Your hand *is* power and might; in Your hand *it is* to make great and to give strength to all" (1 Chronicles 29:12).

20. "The thief does not come except to steal, and to kill, and to destroy. I have come that they may have life, and that they may have *it* more abundantly" (John 10:10).

21. "In Him also we have obtained an inheritance, being predestined according to the purpose of Him who works all things according to the counsel of His will" (Ephesians 1:11).

"And we know that all things work together for good to those who love God, to those who are the called according to *His* purpose. For whom He foreknew, He also predestined *to be* conformed to the image of His Son, that He might be the firstborn among many brethren. Moreover whom He predestined, these He also called; whom He called, these He also justified; and whom He justified, these He also glorified" (Romans 8:28–30).

Chapter Eight: Closing Prayer

1. "Then I heard a loud voice saying in heaven, 'Now salvation, and strength, and the kingdom of our God, and the power of His Christ have come, for the accuser of our brethren, who accused them before our God day and night, has been cast down'" (Revelations 12:10).

2. "Nor give place to the devil" (Ephesians 4:27).

Appendix 1: Quick Directions for an Immanuel Session

1. "I, *even* I, *am* the LORD, and besides Me *there is* no savior" (Isaiah 43:11).

◈ About the Author

Pastor Patti Velotta continues to serve as pastor to Calvary Way International Fellowship (CWIF) as she has for over twenty years. She was ordained in 1992 after receiving her master of divinity in 1991 from Trinity Evangelical Divinity School, where she also served for three years as dean of women and assistant dean of students.

She is president of Three Cord Ministries, Inc., an affiliate of CWIF. This Joy! Books, a division of Three Cord Ministries, published Dr. Karl Lehman's book, *Outsmarting Yourself.*

Pastor Patti teaches the foundational truths of biblical Christian faith. She is a woman called into ministry by Jesus to equip others and to position individuals to build up the body of Christ. She actively follows Jesus as he asks her to teach, preach, and bring healing to his body.

Pastor Patti has been experiencing and practicing a lifestyle of *Immanuel* prayer for ten years. Because of her personal pain she was led to Dr. Karl Lehman, a psychiatrist specializing in brain function as it relates to inner healing and spirituality. Through this divine appointment Pastor Patti experienced deep healing in her personal encounters with Jesus. *Immanuel* prayer changed her life and has become a cornerstone of her Christian faith.

As she ministers, Pastor Patti applies the faith, anointing, and compassion developed through her own healing work. She has not only used this training in her personal healing journey, but she has also integrated it into Calvary Way's services, her pastoral prayer ministry, and her relationships. She now teaches this lifestyle in seminars and in one-on-one training. Her intuitive understanding of the process is mixed with revelation in Scripture. As a pastor-teacher, she has been given an anointing to teach *Immanuel* and to explain the deep things of God in layman's terms.

She has been married for forty-three years to Mike. They have three daughters (Mary, Molly, and Emily), two sons-in-law (Evans and Kevin), and six grandchildren (Aiden, Cole, Anna, Ethan, John-Luke, and Mia).

Pastor Patti Velotta may be reached through Calvary Way International Fellowship, e-mail: calvaryway@aol.com.